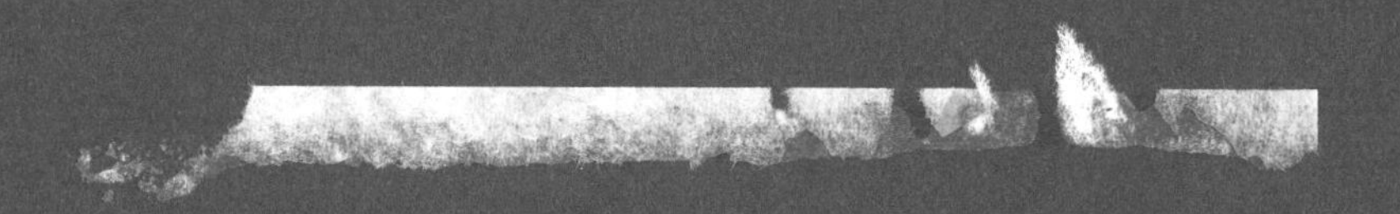

WITHDRAWN FROM STOCK

Step-by-Step

50 Low Fat Sauces

STEP-BY-STEP

50 Low Fat Sauces

Consultant Editor

Linda Fraser

LORENZ BOOKS
LONDON • NEW YORK • SYDNEY • BATH

This edition published in the UK in 1997 by Lorenz Books

Lorenz Books is an imprint of
Anness Publishing Limited
Hermes House
88–89 Blackfriars Road
London SE1 8HA

ISBN 1 85967 426 7

A CIP catalogue record for this book is available from the British Library

Publisher: Joanna Lorenz
Consultant Editor: Linda Fraser
Assistant Editor: Margaret Malone
Recipes: Catherine Atkinson, Nicola Diggins, Christine France, Sue Maggs, Annie Nichols, Liz Trigg and Steven Wheeler
Jacket Designer: Brian Weldon
Designers: Kim Bale, Visual Image, Peter Butler, Bob Gordon, Peter Laws, Alan Marshall and Keith Brambury
Photographers: William Adams-Lingwood, Edward Allwright, James Duncan, Michelle Garrett, Don Last and Peter Reilly

For all recipes, quantities are given in both metric and imperial measures, and, where appropriate, measures are also given in standard cups and spoons. Follow one set, but not a mixture, because they are not interchangeable.

Printed and bound in Hong Kong

1 3 5 7 9 10 8 6 4 2

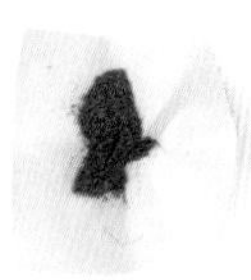

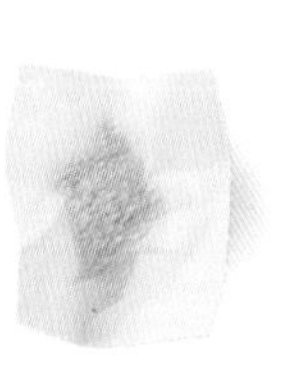

CONTENTS

INTRODUCTION

A delicious sauce, whether served as an accompaniment or as an integral part of a dish, can transform the plain and ordinary into something really exciting. Sauces can also, however, introduce an unwelcome amount of fat into a recipe. It is a common question – how do you cut down on fat without sacrificing flavour? *Step-By-Step 50 Low Fat Sauces* solves this by providing a wealth of fabulous low fat recipes with tips and techniques on quick and easy low fat cooking methods.

Traditionally, sauces frequently include dairy products, such as butter, cream, milk and cheese, or are made with oil and eggs, as in mayonnaise. Sauces made with such ingredients will be high in fat and calories. However, supermarkets now offer a huge selection of reduced fat products that provide ideal alternatives. Yogurt, skimmed or semi-skimmed milk, fromage frais, half fat crème fraîche, reduced-fat spreads and lower-fat soft cheeses like ricotta can all be effortlessly substituted in recipes with delicious, lighter results.

Low fat sauces may also be based on fresh, flavoursome stocks, or fruits and vegetables, cooked if necessary, then puréed or sieved for a smooth consistency. Fragrant fresh herbs, tangy citrus juices, exotic spices and a range of store cupboard ingredients can all be used to create new and imaginative low fat sauces.

Whatever the occasion, from weekday meals to parties and informal entertaining, and whether you need a speedy dip to serve as an easy starter or a light snack, a tasty sauce to jazz up fish, meat, poultry, pasta or vegetables, an exciting Mexican-style salsa accompaniment, or a pretty fruit coulis for a tempting dessert, you'll find an enticing and low fat version here.

Do We Need Fat in Our Diet?

We only need 10 g/¼ oz fat in our daily diet for our bodies to function properly. A totally fat-free diet would be almost impossible to achieve, since some fat is present in virtually every food.

A certain amount of essential fatty acids are necessary in our diet to help our bodies absorb vitamins A, D, E and K as they are fat-soluble and cannot be made by the body. Fat is also needed to make hormones. Recent research has proved that we all eat far too much fat. Doctors now recommend that we limit our fat intake to no more than 30% of our total daily calorie intake, even as low as 25% for a really healthy diet. Some fats in the diet are a contributory factor in heart disease and cancers, such as breast, prostate and colon.

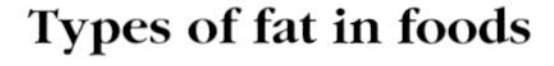

Types of fat in foods

Saturated fats are hard fats found in meat, most dairy products, such as butter, cream, dripping, hard margarines, cheeses and animal fats. Palm and coconut oil are also high in saturated fats. Saturated fats can raise the blood cholesterol level and clog up the arteries. The way we prepare and cook foods can limit the amount of saturated fat that we consume.

Polyunsaturated fats are soft fats such as sunflower, safflower, grapeseed, soya and corn oils, and fish such as mackerel, salmon or herring and nuts, seeds, cereals, lean meats and green vegetables. These fats may help to reduce our cholesterol levels.

Mono-unsaturated fats should make up most of the fat in our diet. They appear to have a protective effect and help lower cholesterol levels. Olive oil, rapeseed oil, peanut oil and avocados are all rich sources of mono-unsaturated fats.

A selection of foods containing the three main types of fat found in foods.

Eating a Healthy Low Fat Diet

Eat a good variety of different foods every day to make sure you get all the nutrients you need.

1 Skimmed milk contains the same amount of calcium, protein and B vitamins as whole milk, but a fraction of the fat.
2 Natural low-fat yogurt, cottage cheese and fromage frais are all high in calcium and protein, and are good substitutes for cream.
3 Starchy foods such as rice, bread, potatoes, cereals and pasta should be eaten at every meal. These foods provide energy and some vitamins, minerals and dietary fibre.
4 Vegetables, salads and fruits should form a major part of the diet, and about 450 g/1 lb should be eaten each day.
5 Eat meat in moderation but eat plenty of fish, particularly oily fish such as mackerel, salmon, tuna, herring and sardines.

A few simple changes to a normal diet can reduce fat intake considerably. The following tips are designed to make the change to a healthier diet as easy as possible.

Meat and poultry
Red meats such as lamb, pork and beef are high in saturated fats, but chicken and turkey contain far less fat. Remove the skin before cooking and trim off any visible fat. Avoid sausages, burgers, patés, bacon and minced beef. Buy lean cuts of meat and skim any fat from the surface of stocks and stews.

Dairy products
Replace whole milk with skimmed or semi-skimmed and use low-fat yogurt, low-fat crème fraîche or fromage frais instead of cream. Eat cream, cream cheese and hard cheeses in moderation. There are reduced-fat cheeses on the market with 14% fat content which is half the fat content of full fat cheese. Use these wherever possible.

Spreads, oils and dressings
Use butter, margarine and low-fat spreads sparingly. Try to avoid using fat and oil for cooking. If you have to use oil, choose olive, corn, sunflower, soya, rapeseed and peanut oils, which are low in saturates. Look out for oil-free dressings and reduced fat mayonnaise.

Hidden fats
Biscuits, cakes, pastries, snacks and processed meals and curries all contain high proportions of fat. Get into the habit of reading food labels carefully and looking for a low-fat option.

Cooking methods
Grill, poach and steam foods whenever possible. If you do fry foods, use as little fat as possible and pat off the excess after browning, with kitchen paper. Make sauces and stews by first cooking the onions and garlic in a small quantity of stock, rather than frying in oil.

A selection of foods for a healthy low-fat diet.

Flavourings for Low Fat Sauces

Sauces don't have to be rich in fat, like the classic mayonnaise, hollandaise and béchamel, or prepared using generous amounts of oil and butter. Take a closer look at the range of readily available ingredients you can use to produce delicious low fat versions.

To compensate for the lack of fat in the form of butter, oil, cream and full-fat cheeses, the recipes in this book make good use of the rich flavours of concentrated sauces, onions, garlic, fresh herbs and spices.

Skimmed milk, yogurt, fromage frais, reduced and lower fat cheeses and spreads have all been used in the recipes to replace higher, full-fat equivalents. This substitution makes considerable fat and calorie savings. Occasionally a small amount of butter is used when the flavour is important to the dish, or perhaps Greek yogurt is recommended rather than a very low fat natural yogurt to add richness to the sauce, but overall there's a significant reduction in fat.

Similarly, hard cheeses such as parmesan and mature or vintage Cheddar are very high in fat, but they also have a wonderful strong flavour, so only a small amount is needed.

Robust ingredients, such as fresh chillies, fresh root ginger, citrus zests and juices, mustards, honey, vinegars, tomato purée, pickles, chutneys and other condiments like soy and hoisin sauce can all be used to create exciting, flavoursome sauces.

Dried mushrooms and sun-dried tomatoes (not the varieties preserved in olive oil) are full of concentrated flavour and add a wonderful richness that really boosts any sauce they are added to.

The aromatic flavours of fresh herbs such as basil, bay leaves, coriander, mint, oregano, parsley, rosemary, sage and thyme can all add their own individual fragrance to sauces, whether as classic partners or used in new and interesting combinations.

The Fat and Calorie Contents of Food

The following figures show the weight of fat (g) and the energy content of 100 g (3½ oz) of each food.

Dairy, Fats, Oils and Eggs	Fat (g)	Energy Kcals/KJ
Milk, whole	3.9	66/275
Milk, semi-skimmed	1.6	46/195
Milk, skimmed	0.1	33/140
Cream, double	48.0	449/1849
Cream, single	19.1	198/817
Soured cream	19.9	205/845
Crème fraîche	40.0	380/1567
Crème fraîche, half fat	15.0	169/700
Buttermilk	0.2	47/198
Cheddar cheese	34.4	412/1708
Cheddar-type, reduced-fat	15.0	261/1091
Parmesan cheese	32.7	452/1880
Edam cheese	25.4	333/1382
Full-fat soft cheese	31.0	313/1293
Medium-fat (light) soft cheese, such as ricotta or curd	14.5	179/743
Quark	0.2	70/293
Cottage cheese, plain	3.9	98/413
Cottage cheese, reduced-fat	1.4	78/331
Fromage frais, plain	7.1	113/469
Fromage frais, very low fat	0.2	58/247
Low fat yogurt, plain	0.8	56/236
Greek-style yogurt	9.1	115/477
Mayonnaise	75.6	691/2843
Mayonnaise, reduced-calorie	36.9	366/1510
Butter	81.7	737/3031
Margarine	81.6	739/3039
Dairy/fat spread	73.4	662/2723
Olive oil (reduced-fat) spread	60.0	544/2242
Low fat spread	40.5	390/1605
Very low fat spread	25.0	273/1128
Corn, Sunflower, Safflower, Soya, Olive oils	99.9	899/3696
Eggs (2 x size 4)	10.8	147/612
Egg yolk	30.5	339/1402
Egg White	Trace	36/153

Information from The Composition of Foods, 5th Edition (1991) is reproduced with the permission of the Royal Society of Chemistry and the Controller of Her Majesty's Stationery Office.

Shopper's Guide to Fats and Spreads

Butter
Must contain at least 80% fat and all the fat must be natural milk fat (full cream). Can be used for spreading, grilling, roasting, shallow and stir-frying, sauces, baking, pastry-making and garnishing.

Margarine
Also must contain 80% fat, no more than 10% of which can be derived from milk. It has the same calorie value as butter. It must also contain added vitamins A and D, which naturally occur in butter. Can be used either for spreading or cooking but doesn't have the same characteristic, creamy buttery flavour.

Polyunsaturated Margarine
Must contain at least 45% polyunsaturated fat but total fat and calorie content is the same as other margarines.

Dairy Spread
A blend of milk fats and vegetable oil. Brands vary in fat and calorie value but are generally slightly lower than butter and margarine. Has the convenience of a spread but can be used in cooking.

Olive Oil Spread
Reduced-fat spread with about 60% fat. It is made with olive oil so is high in monounsaturates and low in saturated fat (the type it's recommended to reduce). Suitable for spreading and stir-frying.

Reduced-Fat Spread
Based on vegetable oil or animal fats and generally about 60% fat, or ¾ that of butter or margarine. Can be used for spreading, baking, stir-frying at a gentle heat and in sauces.

Low Fat Spread/Half Fat Butter Spread
About half the fat (40% content) and calorie value of butter or margarine but with a high moisture content. Suitable for making all-in-one sauces (see below).

Very Low Fat Spread
Made from vegetable oils and various dairy ingredients. Only contains 25% fat, therefore very high moisture content and only suitable for spreading.

Three Healthy Ways to Make Low Fat Sauces

The traditional roux method for making a sauce won't work successfully if using a low fat spread. This is because of the high water content, which will evaporate on heating, leaving insufficient fat to blend with the flour. However, below are three quick and easy low fat alternatives.

1 The All-in-One Method: Place 25 g/1 oz/2 tbsp each of low fat spread and plain flour in a pan with 300 ml/ ½ pint/1 ¼ cups skimmed milk. Bring to the boil, stirring continuously until thickened and smooth. This method is perfect for making a milk-based sauce like cheese or parsley sauce.

2 Using Stock to Replace Fat: Sweat vegetables, such as onions, in a small amount of stock rather than frying in fat.

3 Using Cornflour to Thicken: Rather than using the traditional roux method with fat and flour, blend 15 ml/ 1 tbsp cornflour with 15–30 ml/1–2 tbsp cold water, then whisk into 300 ml/ ½ pint/1 ¼ cups simmering liquid, bring to the boil and cook for 1 minute, stirring continuously.

COOK'S TIP

- Always cook all-in-one sauces over a low heat and whisk or stir constantly. If the sauce looks lumpy, remove from the heat and whisk thoroughly.

How to Adapt Classic Sauces

Mayonnaise
It isn't possible to make low fat mayonnaise at home, but you can buy commercially made reduced-calorie mayonnaise. To make further fat and calorie savings, substitute half the stated quantity with low fat natural yogurt or low fat fromage frais. This works well for mayonnaise-based dips or sauces like Thousand Island, which have tomato purée or ketchup added to the blended mayonnaise and low fat yogurt.

Hollandaise
This sauce is classically made with egg yolks, butter and vinegar. It's not worth making with margarine and it can't be made with low fat spreads. However, some fat saving can be made by using less butter and including buttermilk. Place 3 egg yolks in a bowl with the grated rind and 15 ml/1 tbsp juice from 1 lemon. Heat gently over a pan of water, stirring until thickened. Gradually whisk in 75 g/3 oz/ 6 tbsp softened butter, in small pieces, until smooth. Whisk in 45 ml/3 tbsp buttermilk and season. Reserve for special occasions. Alternatively, flavour plain yogurt with a little French mustard and a little vinaigrette dressing and use to drizzle over asparagus.

Vinaigrette dressings
These are high in fat, even if you use monounsaturated oils, such as olive oil. You can buy reduced-calorie and oil-free dressings or, if you like the real thing, simply use less.

Fat Saving Tips for Making Sauces

- Use skimmed or semi-skimmed milk (if you find the former too thin and watery) in place of whole milk for white sauces.

- Use low fat natural yogurt or half fat crème fraîche in place of cream. If the low fat yogurt or crème fraîche is to be heated, first stir in 30 ml/ 2 tbsp cornflour to stabilize it and prevent the sauce from separating.

- Imitation creams, which are a blend of buttermilk and vegetable oils and which contain less fat than real cream, can be used as a lower-fat alternative in all sorts of sauces.

- Use reduced-fat Cheddar-type cheese or a small amount of parmesan or mature Cheddar for maximum flavour.

- Substitute ricotta, low fat fromage frais, or a skimmed milk soft cheese (such as quark or fromage blanc) in place of full-fat cream cheeses.

- Use a non-stick pan for cooking so less, if any, fat or oil is necessary.

Quick Low-Calorie, Oil-Free Dressings

Whisk together 90 ml/6 tbsp low fat natural yogurt, 30 ml/ 2 tbsp freshly squeezed lemon juice and season to taste with freshly ground black pepper.

If you prefer, wine, cider or fruit vinegar or even orange juice could be used in place of the lemon juice. Add chopped fresh herbs, crushed garlic, mustard, honey, grated horseradish or other flavourings, if you like.

Stocks

Many sauces depend for their depth and richness on a good quality stock base. Fresh stock will give the most balanced flavour and it is worth the effort to make it at home. It may be frozen successfully for several months. Canned beef bouillon and chicken broth are good substitutes. For everyday cooking, most cooks will use stock cubes, but these often have a salt base so taste carefully and season lightly.

FISH STOCK

INGREDIENTS
any fish bones, skin and trimmings available
1 onion
1 carrot
1 celery stick
6 black peppercorns
2 bay leaves
3 parsley stalks

NUTRITIONAL NOTES
PER PORTION:

ENERGY 7 Kcals/31 KJ **FAT** 0.3 g
SATURATED FAT 0 **PROTEIN** 0.7 g
CARBOHYDRATE 0.6 g **FIBRE** 0

1 Peel and coarsely slice the onion. Peel and chop the carrot, and scrub and slice the celery.

2 Place all the ingredients in a large saucepan and add enough water to cover. Bring to the boil, skim the surface and simmer uncovered for 20 minutes.

3 Strain and use immediately or store for two days in the refrigerator.

BROWN STOCK

INGREDIENTS
30 ml/2 tbsp vegetable oil
1.5 kg/3 lb beef bones, cut into pieces
225 g/8 oz shin of beef, cut into pieces
bouquet garni
2 onions, trimmed and quartered
2 carrots, scrubbed and chopped
2 celery sticks, sliced
5 ml/1 tsp black peppercorns
2.5 ml/½ tsp salt

NUTRITIONAL NOTES
PER PORTION:

ENERGY 8 Kcals/33 KJ **FAT** 0.1 g
SATURATED FAT 0 **PROTEIN** 1.3 g
CARBOHYDRATE 0.4 g **FIBRE** 0

1 Drizzle the vegetable oil over the bottom of a roasting tin, add the bones and meat. Coat in oil and bake at 220°C/425°F/Gas 7 for about 20–30 minutes or until well browned, turning regularly during cooking.

2 Transfer the meat and bones to a large saucepan, add the remaining ingredients and cover with 2.5 litres/ 5¾ pints/14 cups of water. Bring to the boil, skim, then partially cover and simmer for 2½–3 hours to reduce by half.

3 Strain the stock into a bowl. Cool and remove the solidified fat before use. Store for up to 4 days in the refrigerator.

CHICKEN OR WHITE STOCK

INGREDIENTS
1 onion
4 cloves
1 carrot
2 leeks
2 celery sticks
1 chicken carcass, cooked or raw, or 750 g/1 1/2 lb veal bones cut into pieces
bouquet garni
8 black peppercorns
2.5 ml/1/2 tsp salt

NUTRITIONAL NOTES
PER PORTION:

ENERGY 8 Kcals/34 KJ **FAT** 0.3 g
SATURATED FAT 0 **PROTEIN** 1.1 g
CARBOHYDRATE 0.3 g **FIBRE** 0

1 Peel the onion, cut into quarters and spike each quarter with a clove. Scrub and roughly chop the vegetables.

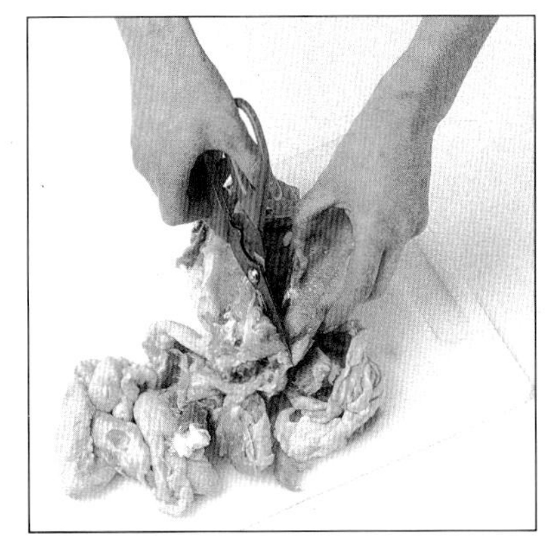

2 Break up the chicken carcass and place in a large saucepan with the remaining ingredients.

3 Cover with 1.7 litres/3 pints/7 cups water. Bring to the boil, skim the surface and simmer, partially covered for 2 hours. Strain the stock into a bowl and allow to cool. When cold remove the hardened fat before using. Store for up to 4 days in the refrigerator.

VEGETABLE STOCK

INGREDIENTS
30 ml/2 tbsp vegetable oil
1 onion
2 carrots
2 large celery sticks, plus any small amounts from the following: leeks, celeriac, parsnip, turnip, cabbage or cauliflower trimmings, mushrooms peelings
bouquet garni
6 black peppercorns

NUTRITIONAL NOTES
PER PORTION:

ENERGY 7 Kcals/28 KJ **FAT** 0.3 g
SATURATED FAT 0 **PROTEIN** 0.3 g
CARBOHYDRATE 0.9 g **FIBRE** 0

1 Peel, halve and slice the onion. Roughly chop the remaining vegetables.

2 Heat the oil in a large pan and fry the onion and vegetables until soft and lightly browned. Add the remaining ingredients and cover with 1.7 litres/3 pints/7 cups water.

3 Bring to the boil, skim the surface then partially cover and simmer for 1 1/2 hours. Strain the stock and allow to cool. Store in the refrigerator for 2–3 days.

Tomato and Dill Dip with Crunchy Baked Mushrooms

This creamy low fat dip is ideal to serve with crispy-coated bites as an informal starter.

NUTRITIONAL NOTES

PER PORTION:

ENERGY 173 Kcals/728 KJ **PROTEIN** 11.88 g
FAT 6.04 g **SATURATED FAT** 3.24 g
CARBOHYDRATE 19.23 g **FIBRE** 1.99 g
ADDED SUGAR 0 **SALT** 0.91 g

Serves 4–6

INGREDIENTS
115 g/4 oz/2 cups fresh fine white breadcrumbs
15 g/½ oz/1½ tbsp finely grated mature Cheddar cheese
5 ml/1 tsp paprika
225 g/8 oz button mushrooms
2 egg whites

FOR THE TOMATO AND DILL DIP
4 ripe tomatoes
115 g/4 oz/½ cup curd cheese
60 ml/4 tbsp natural low fat yogurt
1 garlic clove, crushed
30 ml/2 tbsp chopped fresh dill
salt and freshly ground black pepper
sprig of fresh dill, to garnish

1 Pre-heat the oven to 190°C/375°F/ Gas 5. Mix together the breadcrumbs, cheese and paprika in a bowl.

2 Wipe the mushrooms clean and trim the stalks, if necessary. Lightly whisk the egg whites with a fork, until frothy.

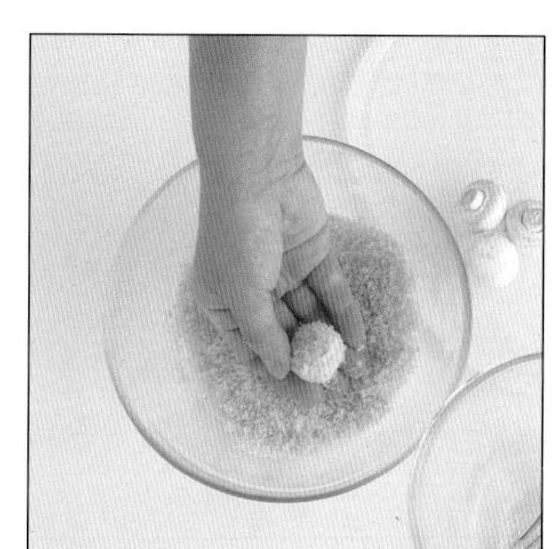

3 Dip each mushroom into the egg whites, then into the breadcrumb mixture. Repeat until all the mushrooms are coated.

4 Put the mushrooms on a non-stick baking sheet. Bake in the pre-heated oven for 15 minutes, or until tender and the coating has turned golden and crunchy.

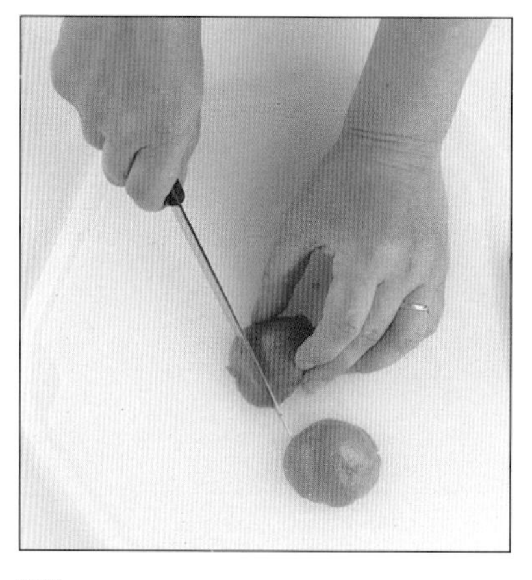

5 Meanwhile, to make the dip, plunge the tomatoes into a saucepan of boiling water for 1 minute, then into a saucepan of cold water. Slip off the skins. Halve, remove the seeds and cores and roughly chop the flesh.

6 Put the curd cheese, yogurt, garlic clove and dill into a mixing bowl and combine well. Season to taste. Stir in the chopped tomatoes. Spoon the mixture into a serving dish and garnish with a sprig of fresh dill. Serve the mushrooms hot, together with the dip.

Garlic and Chilli Dip

This dip is delicious with fresh prawns and other shellfish. It will also spice up any kind of fish when used as an accompanying sauce.

Serves 4

INGREDIENTS
1 small red chilli
2.5 cm/1 in piece root ginger
2 garlic cloves
5 ml/1 tsp mustard powder
15 ml/1 tbsp chilli sauce
30 ml/2 tbsp olive oil
30 ml/2 tbsp light soy sauce
juice of two limes
30 ml/2 tbsp chopped fresh parsley
salt and pepper

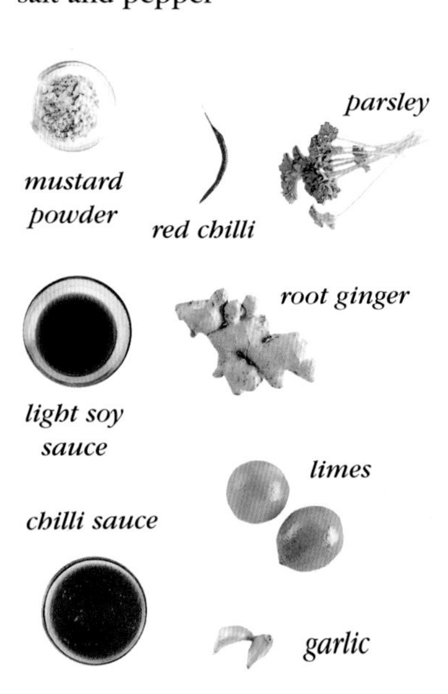

1 Halve the chilli, remove the seeds, stalk and membrane, and chop finely. Peel and roughly chop the ginger.

2 Crush the chilli, ginger, garlic and mustard powder to a paste, using a pestle and mortar.

3 In a bowl, mix together all the remaining ingredients, except the parsley Add the paste and blend it in. Cover and chill for 24 hours.

4 Stir in the parsley and season to taste. It is best to serve in small individual bowls for dipping.

COOK'S TIP

Medium-sized Mediterranean prawns are ideal served with this sauce. Remove the shell but leave the tails intact so there is something to hold on to.

NUTRITIONAL NOTES

PER PORTION:

ENERGY 41 Kcals/171 KJ **FAT** 3.3 g
SATURATED FAT 0.4 g **PROTEIN** 1.2 g
CARBOHYDRATE 1.8 g **FIBRE** 0.4 g

Oriental Hoisin Dip

This speedy Oriental dip needs no cooking and can be made in just a few minutes – it tastes great with mini spring rolls or prawn crackers.

Serves 4

INGREDIENTS
- 4 spring onions
- 4 cm/1½ in piece root ginger
- 2 red chillies
- 2 garlic cloves
- 60 ml/4 tbsp hoisin sauce
- 120 ml/4 fl oz/½ cup passata
- 5 ml/1 tsp sesame oil (optional)

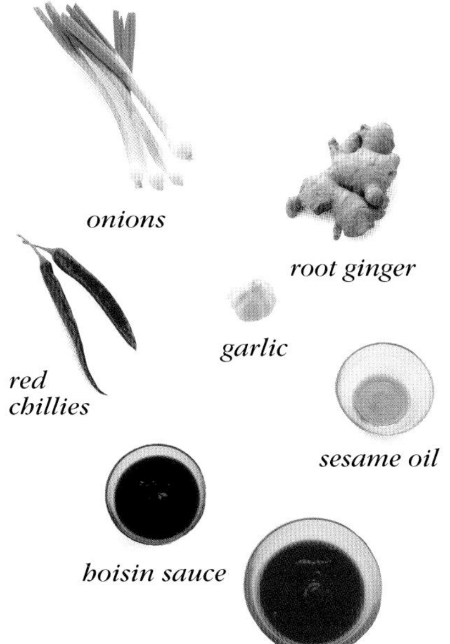

1 Trim off and discard the green ends of the spring onions. Slice the remainder very thinly.

2 Peel the ginger with a swivel-bladed vegetable peeler, then chop it finely.

3 Halve the chillies lengthways and remove their seeds. Finely slice the flesh widthways into tiny strips. Finely chop the garlic.

4 Stir together the hoisin sauce, passata, spring onions, ginger, chilli, garlic and sesame oil, if using, and serve within 1 hour.

COOK'S TIP

Hoisin sauce makes an excellent base for full-flavour dips, especially when combining crunchy vegetables and other Oriental seasonings.

NUTRITIONAL NOTES

PER PORTION:

ENERGY 33 Kcals/140 KJ **FAT** 0.9 g
SATURATED FAT 0.1 g **PROTEIN** 1.3 g
CARBOHYDRATE 5.3 g **FIBRE** 0.4 g

Tsatziki

Serve this classic Greek dip with strips of toasted pitta bread.

Serves 4

Ingredients
1 mini cucumber
4 spring onions
1 garlic clove
200 ml/7 fl oz/scant 1 cup Greek-style yogurt
45 ml/3 tbsp chopped fresh mint
fresh mint sprig, to garnish (optional)
salt and pepper

1 Trim the ends from the cucumber, then cut it into 5 mm/¼ in dice.

2 Trim the spring onions and garlic, then chop both very finely.

3 Beat the yogurt until smooth, if necessary, then gently stir in the cucumber, onions, garlic and mint.

4 Transfer the mixture to a serving bowl and add salt and plenty of freshly ground black pepper to taste. Chill until ready to serve and then garnish with a small mint sprig, if you like.

Cook's Tip

Choose Greek-style yogurt for this dip – it has a higher fat content than most yogurts, but this gives it a deliciously rich, creamy texture.

Nutritional Notes

Per portion:

Energy 65 Kcals/275 KJ **Fat** 4.7 g
Saturated Fat 2.9 g **Protein** 3.9 g
Carbohydrate 2.1 g **Fibre** 0.3 g

Fat-free Saffron Dip

Serve this mild dip with fresh vegetable crudités - it is particularly good with florets of cauliflower.

Serves 4

Ingredients
15 ml/1 tbsp boiling water
small pinch of saffron strands
200 g/7 oz/scant 1 cup fat-free fromage frais
10 fresh chives
10 fresh basil leaves
salt and pepper

1 Pour the boiling water into a small container and add the saffron strands. Leave to infuse for 3 minutes.

2 Beat the fromage frais until smooth, then stir in the infused saffron liquid.

3 Use a pair of scissors to snip the chives into the dip. Tear the basil leaves into small pieces and stir them in.

4 Add salt and pepper to taste. Serve immediately.

Variation

Leave out the saffron and add a squeeze of lemon or lime juice instead.

Nutritional Notes

Per portion:

Energy 29 Kcals/124 KJ **Fat** 0.1 g
Saturated Fat 0.1 g **Protein** 3.9 g
Carbohydrate 3.5 g **Fibre** 0

Watercress and Rocket Sauce with Parsnip Gougères

Nutty puffs with a sweet parsnip centre are the perfect accompaniment to this sauce.

Makes 18 (Serves 6)

INGREDIENTS
115 g/4 oz/½ cup butter
300 ml/½ pint/1¼ cups water
75 g/3 oz/¾ cup plain flour
50 g/2 oz/½ cup wholemeal flour
3 x size 3 eggs, beaten
25 g/1 oz reduced-fat Cheddar cheese, grated
pinch of cayenne pepper or paprika
75 g/3 oz/⅔ cup pecans, chopped
1 medium parsnip, cut into 18 x 2 cm/¾ in pieces
15 ml/1 tbsp skimmed milk
10 ml/2 tsp sesame seeds

FOR THE SAUCE
150 g/5 oz watercress, trimmed
150 g/5 oz rocket, trimmed
175 ml/6 fl oz/¾ cup low fat yogurt
salt, grated nutmeg and freshly ground black pepper
watercress sprigs, to garnish

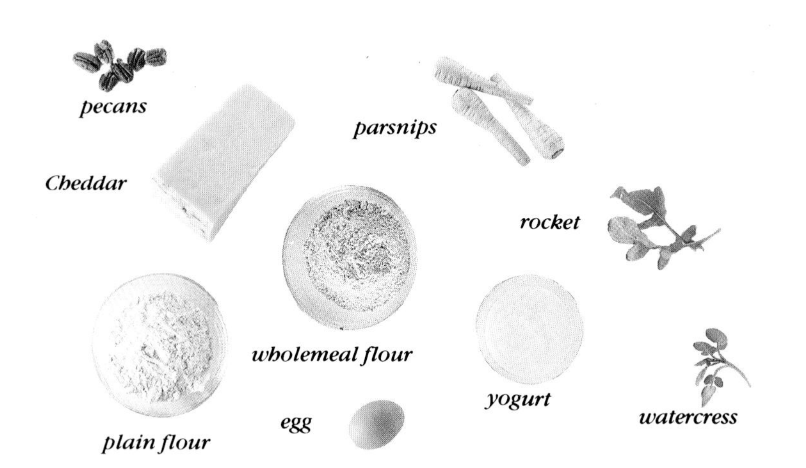

1 Preheat the oven to 200°C/400°F/Gas 6. Place the butter and water in a pan. Bring to the boil and add all the flour in one go. Beat vigorously until the mixture leaves the sides of the pan and forms a ball. Remove from heat and allow the mixture to cool slightly. Beat in the eggs a little at a time until the mixture is shiny and soft enough to fall gently from a spoon.

2 Beat in the Cheddar, cayenne pepper or paprika and the chopped pecans.

3 Lightly grease a baking sheet and drop onto it 18 heaped tablespoons of the mixture. Place a piece of parsnip on each and top with another heaped tablespoon of the mixture.

4 Brush the gougères with a little milk and sprinkle with sesame seeds. Bake in the oven for 25–30 minutes until firm and golden.

Nutritional Notes

Per portion:

Energy 83 Kcals/350 KJ **Fat** 6.1 g
Saturated Fat 2.8 g **Protein** 2.6 g
Carbohydrate 4.9 g **Fibre** 0.7 g

5 Meanwhile make the sauce. Bring a pan of water to the boil and blanch the watercress and rocket for 2–3 minutes. Drain and immediately refresh in cold water. Drain well and chop.

6 Purée the watercress and rocket in a blender or food processor with the yogurt until smooth. Season to taste with salt, nutmeg and freshly ground black pepper. To reheat, place the sauce in a bowl over a gently simmering pan of hot water and heat gently, taking care not to let the sauce curdle. Garnish with watercress.

Creamy Raspberry Dressing with Asparagus

Raspberry vinegar gives this quick low fat dressing a refreshing, tangy flavour – the perfect accompaniment to asparagus.

Serves 4

INGREDIENTS
675 g/1½ lb thin asparagus spears
30 ml/2 tbsp raspberry vinegar
2.5 ml/½ tsp salt
5 ml/1 tsp Dijon-style mustard
60 ml/4 tbsp half fat crème fraîche or natural low fat yogurt
ground white pepper
115 g/4 oz fresh raspberries

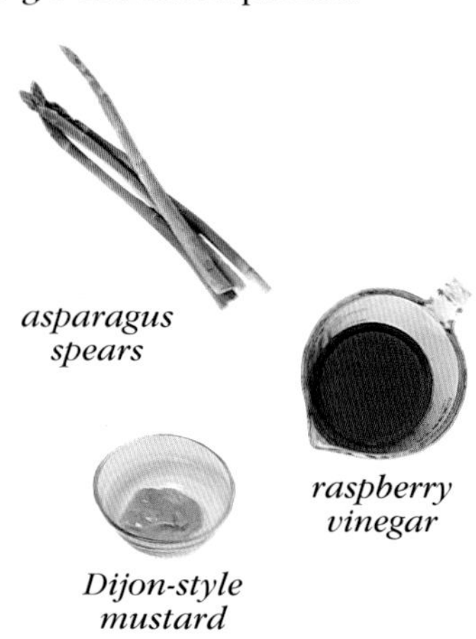

asparagus spears

raspberry vinegar

Dijon-style mustard

half-fat crème fraîche

fresh raspberries

NUTRITIONAL NOTES
PER PORTION:

ENERGY 60 Kcals/251 KJ **FAT** 1.3 g
SATURATED FAT 0.1 g **PROTEIN** 6.2 g
CARBOHYDRATE 6.0 g **FIBRE** 3.6 g

1 Fill a large wide frying pan, or wok, with water about 10 cm/4 in deep and bring to the boil.

2 Trim the tough ends of the asparagus spears. If desired, remove the "scales" using a vegetable peeler.

3 Tie the asparagus spears into two bundles. Lower the bundles into the boiling water and cook for 3–5 minutes, or until just tender.

4 Carefully remove the asparagus bundles from the boiling water using a slotted spoon and immerse them in cold water to stop the cooking. Drain and untie the bundles. Pat dry with kitchen paper. Chill the asparagus for at least 1 hour.

5 Mix together the vinegar and salt in a bowl and stir with a fork until dissolved. Stir in the mustard. Gradually stir in the crème fraîche or yogurt until blended. Add pepper to taste. To serve, place the asparagus on individual plates and drizzle the dressing across the middle of the spears. Garnish with the fresh raspberries and serve at once.

Egg and Lemon Sauce with Leeks

This sauce has a delicious tangy taste and brings out the best in fresh leeks.

Serves 4

INGREDIENTS
675 g/1½ lb baby leeks
15 ml/1 tbsp cornflour
10 ml/2 tsp sugar
1 egg yolk
juice of 1½ lemons
salt

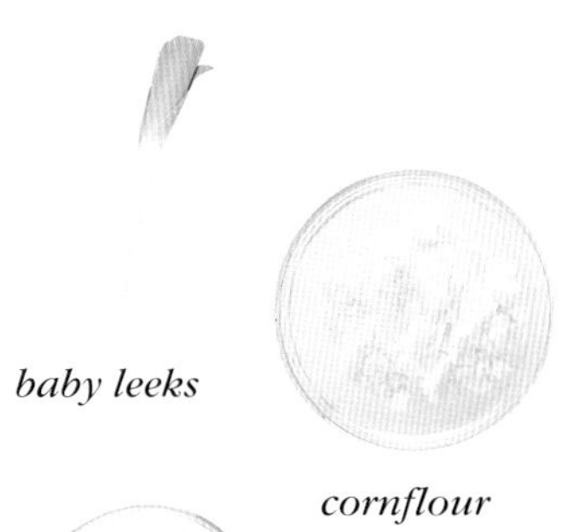

baby leeks

cornflour

sugar

egg

lemons

1 Trim the leeks, slit them from top to bottom and rinse very well under cold water to remove any dirt.

2 Place the leeks in a large saucepan so they lie flat on the base, cover with water and add a little salt. Bring to the boil, cover and gently simmer for 4–5 minutes until just tender.

3 Carefully remove the leeks using a slotted spoon, drain well and arrange in a shallow serving dish. Reserve 200 ml/7 fl oz/scant 1 cup of the cooking liquid.

4 Blend the cornflour with the cooled cooking liquid and place in a small saucepan. Bring to the boil, stirring all the time, and cook over a gentle heat until the sauce thickens slightly. Stir in the sugar and then remove the saucepan from the heat and allow to cool slightly.

5 Beat the egg yolk thoroughly with the lemon juice and stir gradually into the cooled sauce. Cook over a low heat, stirring all the time, until the sauce is fairly thick. Be careful not to overheat the sauce or it may curdle. As soon as the sauce has thickened remove the pan from the heat and continue stirring for a minute. Taste and add salt or sugar as necessary. Cool slightly.

6 Stir the cooled sauce with a wooden spoon. Pour the sauce over the leeks and then cover and chill well for at least 2 hours before serving.

NUTRITIONAL NOTES

PER PORTION:

ENERGY 76 Kcals/320 KJ **FAT** 2.2g
SATURATED FAT 0.4g **PROTEIN** 3.2 g
CARBOHYDRATE 11.7 g **FIBRE** 3.3 g

Spicy Cocktail Dressing with Crab and Pasta Salad

Serves 6

INGREDIENTS
350 g/12 oz fusilli
1 small red pepper, seeded and finely chopped
2 x 175 g/6 oz cans white crab meat, drained
115 g/4 oz cherry tomatoes, halved
¼ cucumber, halved, seeded and sliced into crescents
15 ml/1 tbsp lemon juice
300 ml/½ pint/1¼ cups low-fat yogurt
2 sticks celery, finely chopped
10 ml/2 tsp horseradish cream
2.5 ml/½ tsp ground paprika
2.5 ml/½ tsp Dijon mustard
30 ml/2 tbsp sweet tomato pickle or chutney
salt and ground black pepper
fresh basil, to garnish

1 Cook the pasta in a large pan of boiling, salted water according to the instructions on the packet. Drain and rinse thoroughly under cold water.

2 Cover the chopped red pepper with boiling water and stand for 1 minute. Drain and rinse under cold water. Pat dry on kitchen paper.

NUTRITIONAL NOTES
PER PORTION:

ENERGY 305Kcals/1283KJ **FAT** 2.5g
SATURATED FAT 0.5g **CHOLESTEROL** 43mg
CARBOHYDRATE 53g **FIBRE** 2.9g

3 Drain the crab meat and pick over carefully for pieces of shell. Put into a bowl with the halved tomatoes and sliced cucumber. Season with salt and pepper and sprinkle with lemon juice.

4 To make the dressing, add the red pepper to the yogurt, celery, horseradish, paprika, mustard and sweet tomato pickle or chutney. Mix the pasta with the dressing and transfer to a serving dish. Spoon the crab mixture on top and garnish with fresh basil.

Egg and Lemon Mayonnaise

This recipe draws on the contrasting flavours of egg and lemon, with the chopped parsley providing a fresh finish - perfect for potato salad. Serve with an assortment of cold meats or fish for a simple, tasty meal.

Serves 4

INGREDIENTS
900 g/2 lb new potatoes, scrubbed or scraped
1 medium onion, finely chopped
1 egg, hard-boiled
150 ml/5 fl oz/⅔ cup reduced-calorie mayonnaise
1 garlic clove, crushed
finely grated zest and juice of 1 lemon
60 ml/4 tbsp chopped fresh parsley
salt and pepper

COOK'S TIP

At certain times of the year potatoes are inclined to fall apart when boiled. This usually coincides with the end of a particular season when potatoes become starchy. Early-season varieties are therefore best for making salads.

1 Bring the potatoes to the boil in a saucepan of salted water. Simmer for 20 minutes. Drain and allow to cool. Cut the potatoes into large dice, season well and combine with the onion.

2 Shell the hard-boiled egg and grate into a mixing bowl, then add the mayonnaise. Combine the garlic and lemon zest and juice in a small bowl and stir into the mayonnaise.

3 Fold in the chopped parsley, mix thoroughly into the potatoes and serve.

NUTRITIONAL NOTES

PER PORTION:

ENERGY 303 Kcals/1273 KJ **FAT** 12.9 g
SATURATED FAT 2.1 g **PROTEIN** 6.7 g
CARBOHYDRATE 42.4 g **FIBRE** 3.2 g

Citrus Sauce with Baby Courgettes

If baby courgettes are unavailable, you can use larger ones, but they should be cooked whole.

Serves 4

INGREDIENTS
350 g/12 oz baby courgettes
4 spring onions, finely sliced
2.5 cm/1 in fresh root ginger, grated
30 ml/2 tbsp cider vinegar
15 ml/1 tbsp light soy sauce
5 ml/1 tsp soft light brown sugar
45 ml/3 tbsp vegetable stock
finely grated rind and juice of ½ lemon and ½ orange
5 ml/1 tsp cornflour

1 Cook the courgettes in lightly salted boiling water for 3-4 minutes, or until just tender. Drain well.

2 Meanwhile put all the remaining ingredients, except the cornflour, into a small saucepan and bring to the boil. Simmer for 3 minutes.

3 Blend the cornflour with 10 ml/2 tsp of cold water and add to the sauce. Bring to the boil, stirring continuously, until the sauce has thickened.

4 Pour the sauce over the courgettes and gently heat, shaking the pan to coat evenly. Transfer to a warmed serving dish and serve.

NUTRITIONAL NOTES

PER PORTION:

ENERGY 33 K Cals/138 KJ **PROTEIN** 2.18 g
FAT 0.42 g **SATURATED FAT** 0.09 g
CARBOHYDRATE 5.33 g **FIBRE** 0.92 g
ADDED SUGAR 1.31 g **SALT** 0.55 g

Rich Tomato Sauce

For a full tomato flavour and rich red colour use only really ripe tomatoes. Fresh plum tomatoes are an excellent choice if you can find them.

Serves 4–6

INGREDIENTS
30 ml/2 tbsp olive oil
1 large onion, chopped
2 garlic cloves, crushed
1 carrot, finely chopped
1 celery stick, finely chopped
675 g/1½ lb tomatoes, peeled and chopped
150 ml/¼ pint/⅔ cup red wine
150 ml/¼ pint/⅔ cup vegetable stock
1 bouquet garni
15 ml/1 tbsp tomato purée
2.5–5 ml/½–1 tsp granulated sugar
salt and pepper

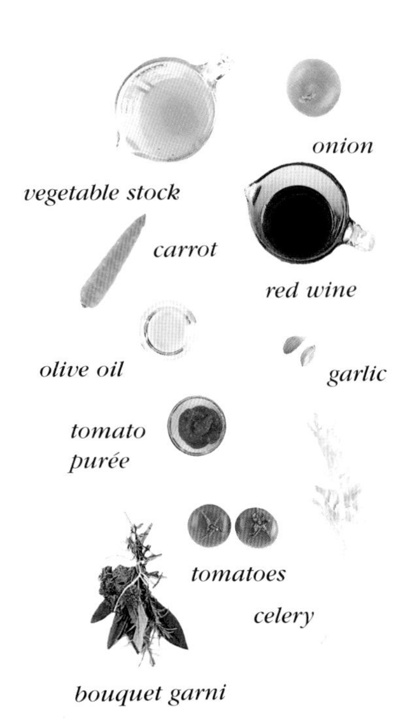

1 Heat the oil and sauté the onion and garlic until soft. Add the carrot and celery and continue to cook, stirring occasionally, until golden.

2 Stir in the tomatoes, wine, stock, bouquet garni and seasoning. Bring to the boil, cover and simmer for 45 minutes, stirring occasionally.

NUTRITIONAL NOTES
PER PORTION:

ENERGY 134 Kcals/564 KJ **FAT** 6.2 g
SATURATED FAT 0.8 g **PROTEIN** 2.4 g
CARBOHYDRATE 11.9 g **FIBRE** 3.0 g

3 Remove the bouquet garni and adjust the seasoning, adding sugar and tomato purée as necessary.

4 Serve the sauce as it is or, for a smoother texture, purée in a blender or food processor, or press through a sieve. Spoon over sliced courgettes or whole round beans.

Mushroom Sauce with Carrot Mousse

Combining this tasty sauce with an impressive, yet easy-to-make, mousse makes healthy eating a pleasure.

NUTRITIONAL NOTES

PER PORTION:

ENERGY 174 K Cals/732 KJ **PROTEIN** 12.65 g
FAT 5.90 g **SATURATED FAT** 1.44 g
CARBOHYDRATE 18.69 g **FIBRE** 3.13 g
ADDED SUGAR 0 **SALT** 0.42 g

Serves 4

INGREDIENTS

350 g/12 oz carrots, roughly chopped
1 small red pepper, seeded and roughly chopped
45 ml/3 tbsp vegetable stock or water
2 eggs
1 egg white
115 g/4 oz/½ cup quark or low fat soft cheese
15 ml/1 tbsp chopped fresh tarragon
salt and freshly ground black pepper
sprig of fresh tarragon, to garnish
boiled rice and leeks, to serve

FOR THE MUSHROOM SAUCE

25 g/1 oz/2 tbsp low fat spread
175 g/6 oz mushrooms, sliced
30 ml/2 tbsp plain flour
250 ml/8 fl oz/1 cup skimmed milk

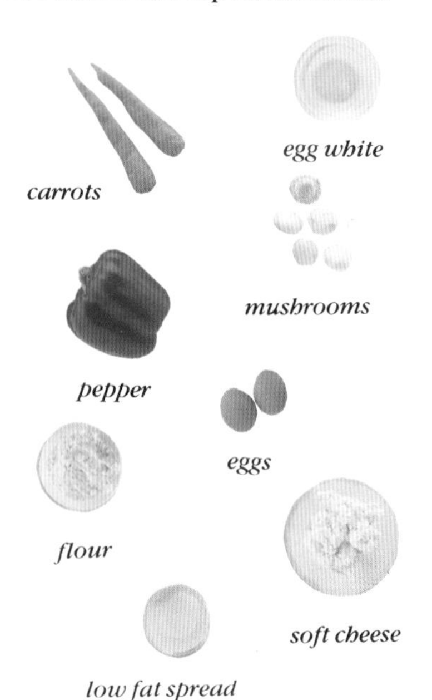

1 Pre-heat the oven to 190°C/375°F/Gas 5. Line the bases of four 150 ml/¼ pint/⅔ cup dariole moulds or ramekin dishes with non-stick baking paper. Put the carrots and red pepper in a small saucepan with the vegetable stock or water. Cover and cook for 5 minutes, or until tender. Drain well.

2 Lightly beat the eggs and egg white together. Mix with the quark or low fat soft cheese. Season to taste. Purée the cooked vegetables in a food processor or blender. Add the cheese mixture and process for a few seconds more until smooth. Stir in the chopped tarragon.

3 Divide the carrot mixture between the prepared dariole moulds or ramekin dishes and cover with foil. Place the dishes in a roasting tin half-filled with hot water. Bake in the pre-heated oven for 35 minutes, or until set.

4 For the mushroom sauce, melt 15 g/½ oz/1 tbsp of the low fat spread in a frying pan. Add the mushrooms and gently sauté for 5 minutes, until soft.

5 Put the remaining low fat spread in a small saucepan together with the flour and milk. Cook over a medium heat, stirring all the time, until the sauce thickens. Stir in the mushrooms and season to taste.

6 Turn out each mousse onto a serving plate. Spoon over a little sauce and serve the remainder separately. Garnish with a sprig of fresh tarragon and serve with boiled rice and leeks.

Quick Tomato Sauce with Fish Balls

This quick sauce is ideal to serve with fish balls and makes a good choice for children. If you like, add a dash of chilli sauce.

Serves 4

INGREDIENTS
450 g/1 lb hoki or other white fish fillets, skinned
60 ml/4 tbsp fresh wholemeal breadcrumbs
30 ml/2 tbsp snipped chives or spring onions
400 g/14 oz can chopped tomatoes
50 g/2 oz/¾ cup button mushrooms, sliced
salt and pepper

1 Cut the fish fillets into fairly large chunks and place in a food processor. Add the wholemeal breadcrumbs and chives or spring onions. Season to taste with salt and pepper and process until the fish is finely chopped but still has some texture left.

2 Divide the fish mixture into about 16 even-size pieces, then mould them into balls with your hands.

3 Place the tomatoes and mushrooms in a wide saucepan and cook over a medium heat until boiling. Add the fish balls, cover and simmer for about 10 minutes, until cooked. Serve hot.

Cook's Tip

Hoki is a good choice for this dish but if it's not available, use cod, haddock or whiting instead.

Nutritional Notes

Per portion:

Energy 137 Kcals/573 KJ **Fat** 1.4 g
Saturated Fat 0.2 g **Protein** 22.3 g
Carbohydrate 9.4 g **Fibre** 1.8 g

Warm Green Tartare Sauce with Seafood

Serves 4

INGREDIENTS
120 ml/4 fl oz/½ cup half fat creme fraiche
10 ml/2 tsp wholegrain mustard
2 garlic cloves, crushed
30-45 ml/2-3 tbsp fresh lime juice
60 ml/4 tbsp chopped fresh parsley
30 ml/2 tbsp snipped chives
350 g/12 oz black tagliatelle
12 large scallops
60 ml/4 tbsp white wine
150 ml/¼ pint/⅔ cup fish stock
salt and ground black pepper
lime wedges and parsley sprigs, to garnish

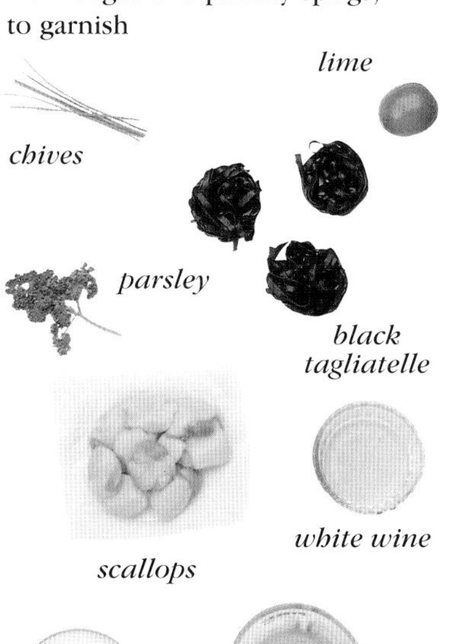

1 To make the tartare sauce, mix the crème fraîche, mustard, garlic, lime juice, herbs and seasoning together in a bowl.

2 Cook the pasta in a large pan of boiling, salted water until *al dente*. Drain thoroughly.

3 Slice the scallops in half, horizontally. Keep any coral whole. Put the white wine and fish stock into a saucepan. Heat to simmering point. Add the scallops and cook very gently for 3–4 minutes (no longer or they will become tough).

4 Remove the scallops. Boil the wine and stock to reduce by half and add the green sauce to the pan. Heat gently to warm, replace the scallops and cook for 1 minute. Spoon over the pasta and garnish with lime wedges and parsley.

NUTRITIONAL NOTES
PER PORTION:

ENERGY 433Kcals/1820KJ **FAT** 3.4g
SATURATED FAT 0.6g **CHOLESTEROL** 45mg
CARBOHYDRATE 68g **FIBRE** 3.4g

Lemon and Chive Sauce with Herby Fishcakes

This tangy sauce makes a delicious accompaniment to fishcakes.

Serves 4

INGREDIENTS
350 g/12 oz potatoes, peeled
75 ml/5 tbsp skimmed milk
350 g/12 oz haddock or hoki fillets, skinned
15 ml/1 tbsp lemon juice
15 ml/1 tbsp creamed horseradish sauce
30 ml/2 tbsp chopped fresh parsley
flour, for dusting
115 g/4 oz/2 cups fresh wholemeal breadcrumbs
salt and freshly ground black pepper
sprig of flat-leaf parsley, to garnish
mange tout and a sliced tomato and onion salad, to serve

FOR THE LEMON AND CHIVE SAUCE
thinly pared rind and juice of ½ small lemon
120 ml/4 fl oz/½ cup dry white wine
2 thin slices fresh root ginger
10 ml/2 tsp cornflour
30 ml/2 tbsp snipped fresh chives

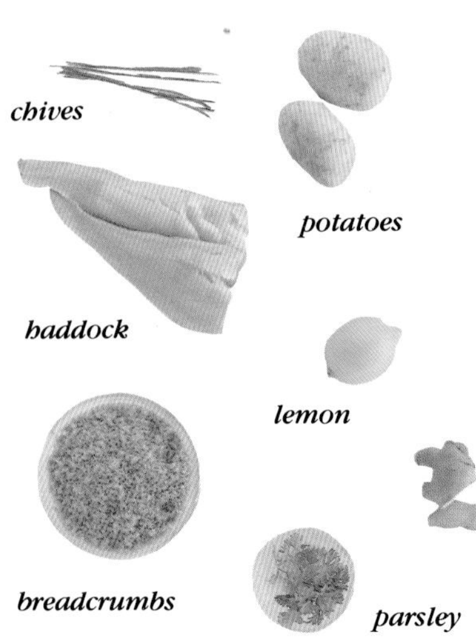

1 Cook the potatoes in a large saucepan of boiling water for 15-20 minutes. Drain and mash with the milk and season to taste.

2 Purée the fish together with the lemon juice and horseradish sauce in a blender or food processor. Mix together with the potatoes and parsley.

3 With floured hands, shape the mixture into eight fishcakes and coat with the breadcrumbs. Chill in the refrigerator for 30 minutes.

4 Cook the fishcakes under a pre-heated moderate grill for 5 minutes on each side, until browned.

5 To make the sauce, cut the lemon rind into julienne strips and put into a large saucepan together with the lemon juice, wine and ginger and season to taste.

NUTRITIONAL NOTES

PER PORTION:

ENERGY 232 Kcals/975 KJ **PROTEIN** 19.99 g
FAT 1.99 g **SATURATED FAT** 0.26 g
CARBOHYDRATE 30.62 g **FIBRE** 3.11 g
ADDED SUGAR 0 **SALT** 0.82 g

6 Simmer uncovered for 6 minutes. Blend the cornflour with 15 ml/1 tbsp of cold water. Add to the saucepan and simmer until clear. Stir in the chives immediately before serving. Serve the sauce hot with the fishcakes, garnished with sprigs of flat-leaf parsley and accompanied with mange tout and a sliced tomato and onion salad.

Parsley Sauce with Smoked Haddock and Pasta

Serves 4

INGREDIENTS
450 g/1 lb smoked haddock fillet
1 small leek or onion, sliced thickly
300 ml/½ pint/1¼ cups skimmed milk
a bouquet garni (bay leaf, thyme and parsley stalks)
25 g/1 oz low-fat margarine
25 g/1 oz plain flour
30 ml/2 tbsp chopped fresh parsley
225 g/8 oz pasta shells
salt and ground black pepper
15 g/½ oz toasted flaked almonds, to serve

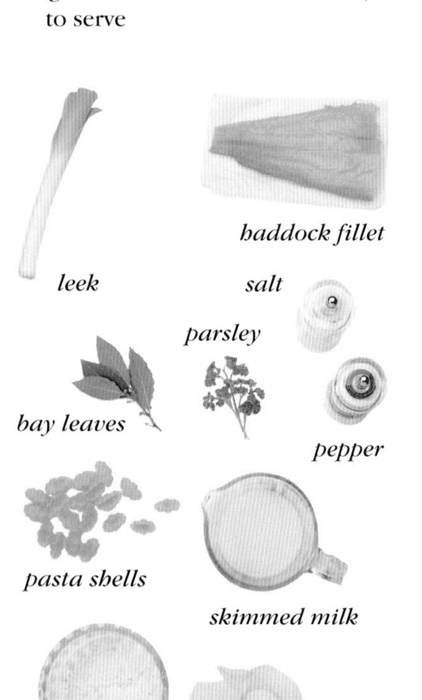

1 Remove all the skin and any bones from the haddock. Put into a pan with the leek or onion, milk and bouquet garni. Bring to the boil, cover and simmer gently for about 8–10 minutes until the fish flakes easily.

2 Strain, reserving the milk for making the sauce, and discard the bouquet garni.

NUTRITIONAL NOTES

PER PORTION:

ENERGY 405Kcals/1700KJ **FAT** 6.9g
SATURATED FAT 1.0g **CHOLESTEROL** 42mg
CARBOHYDRATE 58g **FIBRE** 3.7g

3 Put the margarine, flour and reserved milk into a pan. Bring to the boil and whisk until smooth. Season and add the fish and leek or onion.

4 Cook the pasta in a large pan of boiling water until *al dente*. Drain thoroughly and stir into the sauce with the chopped parsley. Serve immediately, scattered with almonds.

Sorrel Sauce with Salmon Steaks

The sharp flavour of the sorrel sauce balances the richness of the fish. If sorrel is not available, use finely chopped watercress instead.

Serves 2

INGREDIENTS

2 salmon steaks (about 250 g/ 9 oz each)
5 ml/1 tsp olive oil
15 g/½ oz/1 tbsp butter
2 shallots, finely chopped
45 ml/3 tbsp half fat crème fraîche
100 g/3½ oz fresh sorrel leaves, washed and patted dry
salt and pepper
fresh sage, to garnish

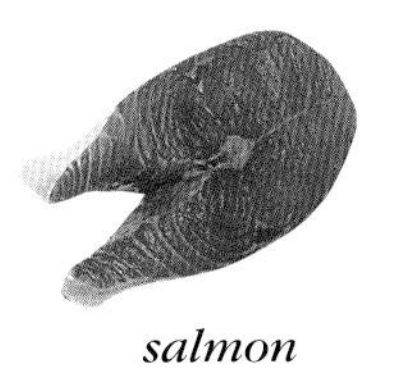

salmon

olive oil

shallots

butter

half fat crème fraîche

sorrel leaves

sage

1 Season the salmon steaks with salt and pepper. Brush a non-stick frying pan with the oil.

2 In a small saucepan, melt the butter over a medium heat. Add the shallots and fry for 2–3 minutes, stirring frequently, until just softened.

3 Add the crème fraîche and the sorrel to the shallots and cook until the sorrel is completely wilted, stirring constantly.

4 Meanwhile, place the frying pan over a medium heat until hot.

COOK'S TIP

If preferred, cook the salmon steaks in a microwave oven for about 4–5 minutes, tightly covered, or according to the manufacturer's guidelines.

5 Add the salmon steaks and cook for about 5 minutes, turning once, until the flesh is opaque next to the bone. If you're not sure, pierce with the tip of a sharp knife; the juices should run clear.

6 Arrange the salmon steaks on two warmed plates, garnish with sage and serve with the sorrel sauce.

NUTRITIONAL NOTES

PER PORTION:

ENERGY 86 Kcals/362 KJ **FAT** 6.8 g
SATURATED FAT 3.9 g **PROTEIN** 3.7 g
CARBOHYDRATE 2.8 g **FIBRE** 1.0 g

Mexican Barbecue Sauce

This spicy, tomato and mustard sauce is delicious served with char-grilled salmon fillets – cook them either on a barbecue or under a hot grill.

Serves 4

NUTRITIONAL NOTES

PER PORTION:

ENERGY 125 Kcals/525 KJ **FAT** 3.5 g
SATURATED FAT 1.4 g **PROTEIN** 2.8 g
CARBOHYDRATE 21.9 g **FIBRE** 1.6 g

INGREDIENTS

1 small red onion
1 garlic clove
6 plum tomatoes
10 ml/2 tsp butter
45 ml/3 tbsp tomato ketchup
30 ml/2 tbsp Dijon mustard
30 ml/2 tbsp dark brown sugar
15 ml/1 tbsp runny honey
5 ml/1 tsp ground cayenne pepper
15 ml/1 tbsp ancho chilli powder
15 ml/1 tbsp ground paprika
15 ml/1 tbsp Worcestershire sauce
4 x 175 g/6 oz salmon fillets

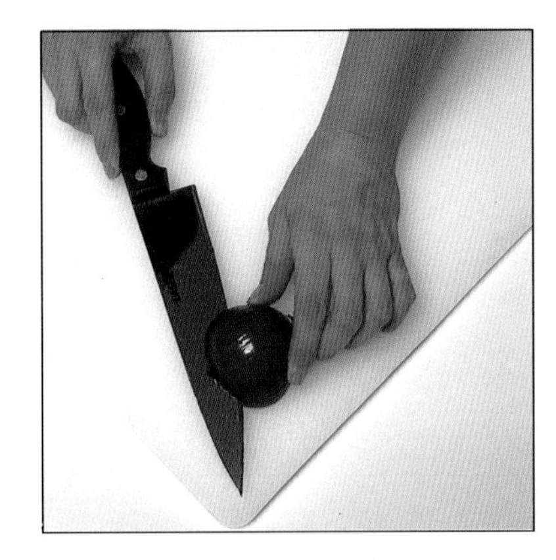

1 Finely chop the red onion and finely dice the garlic.

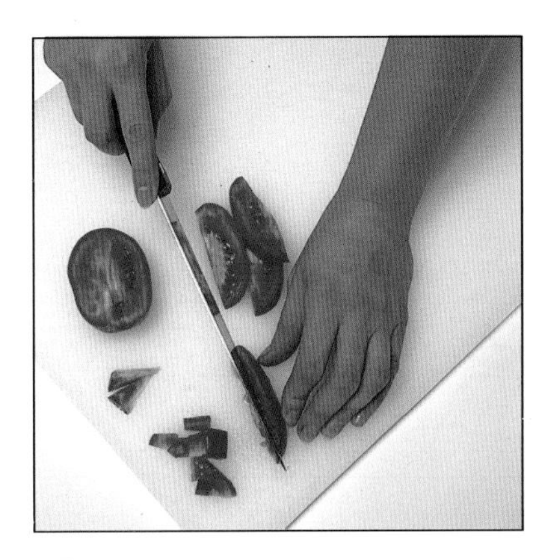

2 Dice the tomatoes.

3 Melt the butter in a large, heavy-based saucepan and gently cook the onion and garlic until translucent.

4 Add the tomatoes and simmer for 15 minutes.

5 Add the remaining ingredients except the salmon and simmer for a further 20 minutes. Process the mixture in a food processor fitted with a metal blade and leave to cool.

6 Brush the salmon with the sauce and chill for at least 2 hours. Barbecue or grill for about 2–3 minutes either side, brushing on the sauce when necessary.

Cranberry Sauce

This is the sauce for roast turkey, but don't just keep it for festive occasions. The vibrant colour and tart taste are a perfect partner to any white roast meat, and it makes a great addition to a chicken sandwich.

Serves 6

INGREDIENTS
1 orange
225 g/8 oz/2 cups fresh or frozen cranberries
250 g/9 oz/1¼ cups granulated sugar

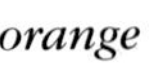

orange

granulated sugar

cranberries

1 Pare the rind thinly from the orange, taking care not to remove any white pith. Squeeze the juice.

2 Place in a saucepan with the cranberries, sugar and 150 ml/¼ pint/⅔ cup water.

3 Bring to the boil, stirring until the sugar has dissolved, then simmer for 10–15 minutes or until the berries burst.

4 Remove the rind and allow to cool before serving.

NUTRITIONAL NOTES

PER PORTION:

ENERGY 163 Kcals/686 KJ **FAT** 0.1 g
SATURATED FAT 0 **PROTEIN** 0.4 g
CARBOHYDRATE 42.9 g **FIBRE** 1.6 g

Mint Sauce

Tart, yet sweet, this simple sauce is the perfect foil to rich meat. It's best served, of course, with new season's roast lamb, but is wonderful, too, with grilled lamb chops or pan-fried duck.

Serves 6

INGREDIENTS
small bunch of mint
15 ml/1 tbsp granulated sugar
30 ml/2 tbsp boiling water
45 ml/3 tbsp white wine vinegar

white wine vinegar

mint

sugar

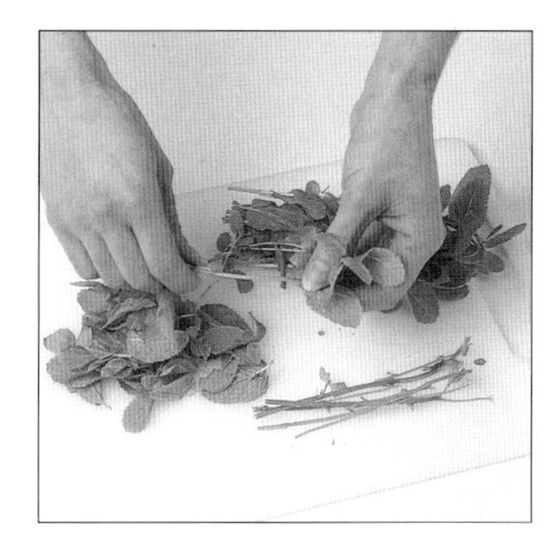

1 Strip the leaves from the stalks.

2 Chop the leaves very finely.

3 Place in a bowl with the sugar and pour on the boiling water. Stir well and let stand for 5–10 minutes.

4 Add the vinegar and let stand for 1–2 hours before serving.

NUTRITIONAL NOTES
PER PORTION:

ENERGY 12 Kcals/50 KJ **FAT** 0.1 g
SATURATED FAT 0 **PROTEIN** 0.2 g
CARBOHYDRATE 2.9 g **FIBRE** 0

Barbecue Sauce

Brush this sauce liberally over chicken drumsticks, chops or kebabs before cooking on the barbecue, or serve as a hot or cold accompaniment to hot dogs and burgers.

Serves 4

INGREDIENTS
10 ml/2 tsp vegetable oil
1 large onion, chopped
2 garlic cloves, crushed
400 g/14 oz can tomatoes
30 ml/2 tbsp Worcestershire sauce
15 ml/1 tbsp white wine vinegar
45 ml/3 tbsp honey
5 ml/1 tsp mustard powder
2.5 ml/½ tsp chilli seasoning or mild chilli powder
salt and pepper

1 Heat the oil and fry the onions and garlic until soft.

2 Stir in the remaining ingredients and simmer, uncovered, for 15–20 minutes stirring occasionally. Cool slightly.

NUTRITIONAL NOTES

PER PORTION:

ENERGY 102 Kcals/428 KJ **FAT** 2.1 g
SATURATED FAT 0.2 g **PROTEIN** 2.8 g
CARBOHYDRATE 19.3 g **FIBRE** 1.4 g

3 Pour into a food processor or blender and process until smooth.

4 Press through a sieve if you prefer and adjust the seasoning.

Sweet Yellow Pepper Sauce

Yellow peppers make a colourful low fat sauce to serve with stuffed turkey escalopes.

Serves 4

INGREDIENTS
10 ml/2 tsp olive oil
2 large yellow peppers, seeded and chopped
1 small onion, chopped
15 ml/1 tbsp freshly squeezed orange juice
300 ml/½ pint/1¼ cups chicken stock
4 turkey escalopes
75 g/3 oz reduced-fat soft cheese
12 fresh basil leaves
salt and pepper

1 To make yellow pepper sauce, heat half the oil in a pan and gently fry the peppers and onion until beginning to soften. Add the orange juice and stock and cook until very soft.

2 Meanwhile, lay the turkey escalopes out flat and beat them out lightly. Spread the turkey escalopes with the reduced-fat soft cheese. Chop half the basil and sprinkle on top, then roll up, tucking in the ends like an envelope, and secure neatly with half a cocktail stick.

3 Heat the remaining oil in a frying pan and fry the escalopes for 7–8 minutes, turning them frequently, until golden brown and cooked.

4 While the escalopes are cooking, press the pepper mixture through a sieve, or blend until smooth, then strain back into the pan. Season to taste and warm through, or serve cold, with the escalopes, garnished with the remaining basil leaves.

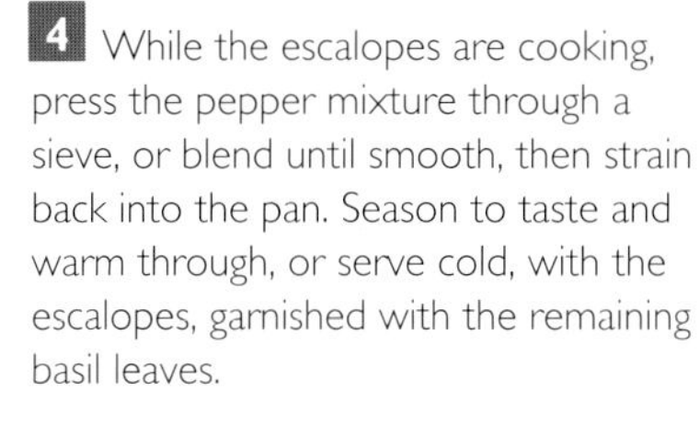

COOK'S TIP

Chicken breast fillets or veal escalopes could be used in place of the turkey.

NUTRITIONAL NOTES

PER PORTION:

ENERGY 186 Kcals/782 KJ **FAT** 3.1 g
SATURATED FAT 0.7 g **PROTEIN** 33.2 g
CARBOHYDRATE 6.6 g **FIBRE** 1.5 g

Herby Yogurt Dressing

Serves 6

INGREDIENTS
450 g/1 lb beef fillet
450 g/1 lb fresh tagliatelle with sun-dried tomatoes and herbs
115 g/4 oz cherry tomatoes
½ cucumber

MARINADE
15 ml/1 tbsp soy sauce
15 ml/1 tbsp sherry
5 ml/1 tsp root ginger, grated
1 garlic clove, crushed

HERB DRESSING
30–45 ml/2–3 tbsp horseradish sauce
150 ml/¼ pint/⅔ cup low-fat yogurt
1 garlic clove, crushed
30–45 ml/2–3 tbsp chopped fresh herbs (chives, parsley, thyme)
salt and ground black pepper

1 Mix all the marinade ingredients together in a shallow dish, put the beef in and turn it over to coat it. Cover with clear film and leave for 30 minutes to allow the flavours to penetrate the meat.

2 Preheat the grill. Lift the fillet out of the marinade and pat it dry with kitchen paper. Place on a grill rack and grill for 8 minutes on each side, basting with the marinade during cooking.

3 Transfer to a plate, cover with foil and leave to stand for 20 minutes.

4 Put all the dressing ingredients into a bowl and mix thoroughly together. Cook the pasta according to the directions on the packet, drain thoroughly, rinse under cold water and leave to dry.

5 Cut the cherry tomatoes in half. Cut the cucumber in half lengthways, scoop out the seeds with a teaspoon and slice thinly into crescents.

6 Put the pasta, cherry tomatoes, cucumber and dressing into a bowl and toss to coat. Slice the beef thinly and arrange on a plate with the pasta salad.

NUTRITIONAL NOTES
PER PORTION:

ENERGY 374Kcals/1572KJ **FAT** 5.7g
SATURATED FAT 1.7g **CHOLESTEROL** 46mg
CARBOHYDRATE 57g **FIBRE** 2.9g

Tomato and Rice Sauce with Turkey Meatballs

Meatballs simmered with rice in a tomato sauce.

COOK'S TIP

To make carrot and courgette ribbons, cut the vegetables lengthways into thin strips using a vegetable peeler, and blanch or steam until cooked through.

NUTRITIONAL NOTES

PER PORTION:

ENERGY 190 Kcals/798 KJ **PROTEIN** 18.04 g
FAT 1.88 g **SATURATED FAT** 0.24 g
CARBOHYDRATE 26.96 g **FIBRE** 1.04 g
ADDED SUGAR 0 **SALT** 0.32 g

Serves 4

INGREDIENTS

25 g/1 oz white bread, crusts removed
30 ml/2 tbsp skimmed milk
1 garlic clove, crushed
2.5 ml/½ tsp caraway seeds
225 g/8 oz minced turkey
1 egg white
350 ml/12 fl oz/1½ cups chicken stock
400 g/14 oz can plum tomatoes
15 ml/1 tbsp tomato purée
90 g/3½ oz/½ cup easy-cook rice
salt and freshly ground black pepper
15 ml/1 tbsp chopped fresh basil, to garnish
carrot and courgette ribbons, to serve

minced turkey

basil

rice

bread

tomato purée

plum tomatoes

caraway seeds

garlic

1 Cut the bread into small cubes and put into a mixing bowl. Sprinkle over the milk and leave to soak for 5 minutes.

2 Add the garlic clove, caraway seeds, turkey, salt and freshly ground black pepper to the bread. Mix together well.

3 Whisk the egg white until stiff, then fold, half at a time, into the turkey mixture. Chill for 10 minutes in the refrigerator.

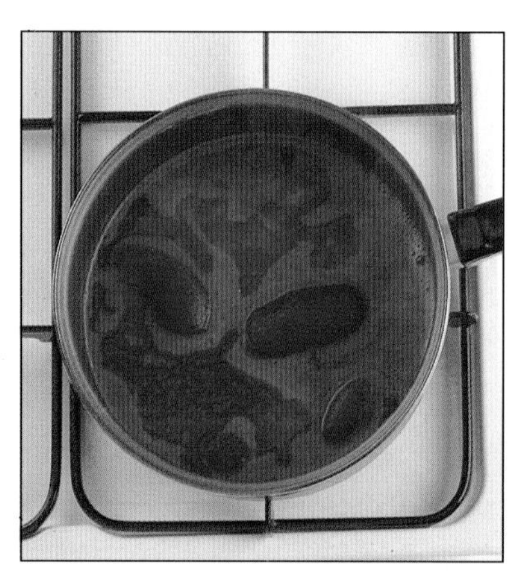

4 Put the stock, tomatoes and tomato purée into a large, heavy-based saucepan and bring to the boil.

5 Add the rice, stir and cook briskly for about 5 minutes. Turn the heat down to a gentle simmer.

6 Meanwhile, shape the turkey mixture into 16 small balls. Carefully drop them into the tomato stock and simmer for a further 8-10 minutes, or until the turkey balls and rice are cooked. Garnish with chopped basil, and serve with carrot and courgette ribbons.

Creamy Orange Sauce with Chicken

This sauce is deceptively creamy – in fact it is made with low fat fromage frais, which is virtually fat-free. The brandy adds a richer flavour, but is optional.

Serves 4

INGREDIENTS
8 chicken drumsticks or thighs, skinned
45 ml/3 tbsp brandy
300 ml/½ pint/1¼ cups orange juice
3 spring onions, chopped
10 ml/2 tsp cornflour
90 ml/6 tbsp low fat fromage frais
salt and pepper

1 Fry the chicken pieces without fat in a non-stick or heavy pan, turning until evenly browned.

2 Stir in the brandy, orange juice and spring onions. Bring to the boil, then cover and simmer for 15 minutes, or until the chicken is tender and the juices run clear, not pink, when pierced.

3 Blend the cornflour with a little water then mix into the fromage frais. Stir this into the sauce and stir over a moderate heat until boiling.

4 Adjust the seasoning and serve with boiled rice or pasta and green salad.

NUTRITIONAL NOTES

PER PORTION:

ENERGY 224 Kcals/942 KJ **FAT** 6.7 g
SATURATED FAT 2.2 g **PROTEIN** 25.2 g
CARBOHYDRATE 10.1 g **FIBRE** 0.2 g

COOK'S TIP

Cornflour stabilizes the fromage frais and helps prevent it curdling.

Sage and Orange Sauce with Pork Fillet

Sage is often partnered with pork – there seems to be a natural affinity – and the addition of orange to the sauce balances the flavour.

Serves 4

INGREDIENTS
2 pork fillets, about 350 g/ 12 oz each
10 ml/2 tsp unsalted butter
120 ml/4 fl oz/½ cup dry sherry
175 ml/6 fl oz/¾ cup chicken stock
2 garlic cloves, very finely chopped
grated rind and juice of 1 unwaxed orange
3 or 4 sage leaves, finely chopped
10 ml/2 tsp cornflour
salt and pepper
orange wedges and sage leaves, to garnish

NUTRITIONAL NOTES
PER PORTION:

ENERGY 330 Kcals/1384 KJ **FAT** 14.6 g
SATURATED FAT 5.8 g **PROTEIN** 36.8 g
CARBOHYDRATE 4.4 g **FIBRE** 0.1 g

1 Season the pork fillets lightly with salt and pepper. Melt the butter in a heavy flameproof casserole over a medium-high heat, then add the meat and cook for 5–6 minutes, turning to brown all sides evenly.

2 Add the sherry, boil for about 1 minute, then add the stock, garlic, orange rind and sage. Bring to the boil and reduce the heat to low, then cover and simmer for 20 minutes, turning once. The meat is cooked if the juices run clear when the meat is pierced with a knife or a meat thermometer inserted into the thickest part of the meat registers 66°C/150°F.

3 Transfer the pork to a warmed platter and cover to keep warm.

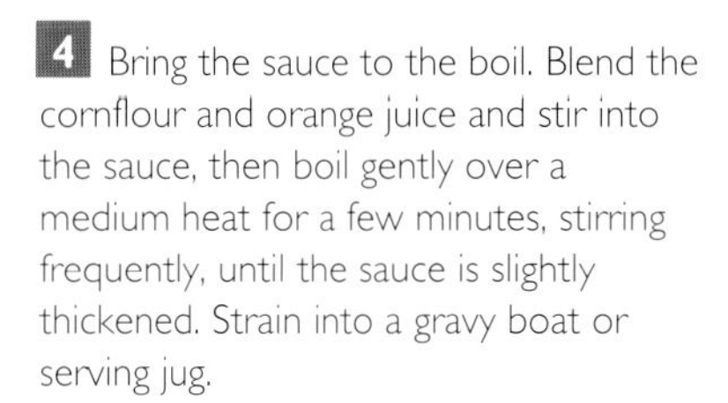

4 Bring the sauce to the boil. Blend the cornflour and orange juice and stir into the sauce, then boil gently over a medium heat for a few minutes, stirring frequently, until the sauce is slightly thickened. Strain into a gravy boat or serving jug.

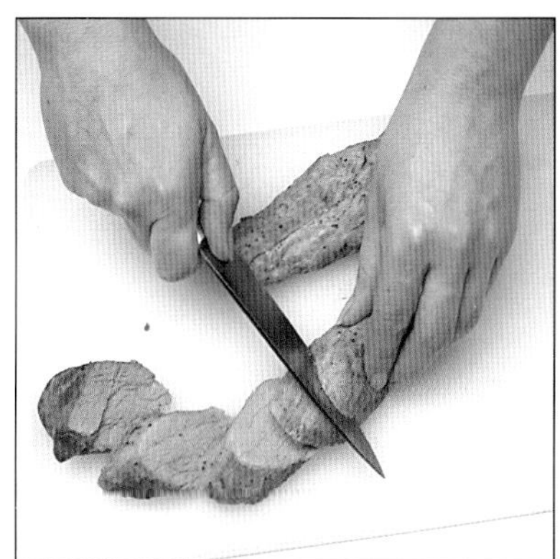

5 Slice the pork diagonally and pour the meat juices into the sauce. Spoon a little sauce over the pork and garnish with orange wedges and sage leaves. Serve the remaining sauce separately.

Cool Mint Raita

The ideal antidote to any spicy food, especially fiery Indian curries.

Serves 4

INGREDIENTS
6 large mint sprigs
1 small onion
½ cucumber
300 ml/½ pint/1¼ cups natural yogurt
2.5 ml/½ tsp salt
2.5 ml/½ tsp sugar
pinch chilli powder
mint sprig, to garnish

1 Tear the mint leaves from their stalks and chop finely.

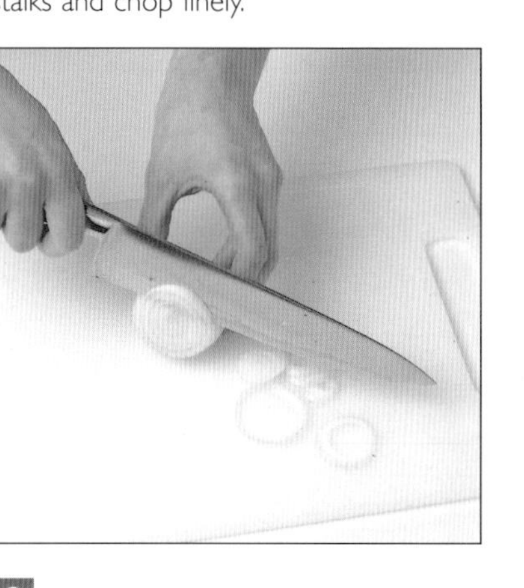

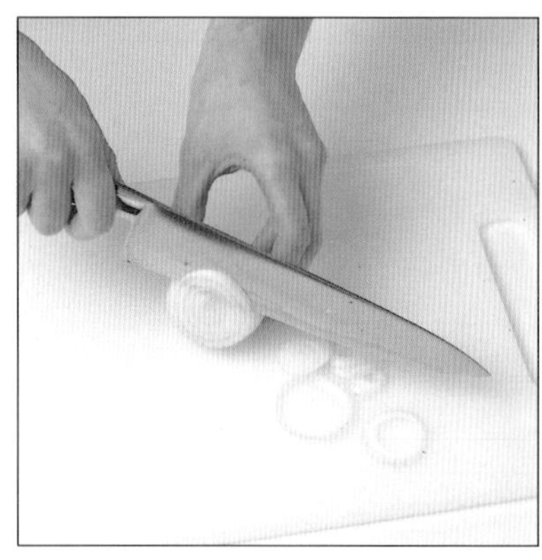

2 Peel and very thinly slice the onion, separating it into rings. Cut the cucumber into 5 mm/¼ in dice.

3 Mix together the mint, onion, cucumber, yogurt, salt and sugar. Spoon into a serving bowl and chill.

4 Just before serving sprinkle with chilli powder and garnish with mint.

VARIATION

This also makes a deliciously fresh dip for crudites, for a creamier texture use Greek yogurt, and add some crushed garlic for extra flavour. Serve with fresh vegetables or tortilla chips.

NUTRITIONAL NOTES

PER PORTION:

ENERGY 54 Kcals/225 KJ **FAT** 0.9 g
SATURATED FAT 0.5 g **PROTEIN** 4.4 g
CARBOHYDRATE 7.6 g **FIBRE** 0.6 g

Chinese-style Sweet and Sour Sauce

A great family favourite that adds a taste of the Orient.

Serves 4

INGREDIENTS
1 carrot
1 green pepper
15 ml/1 tbsp vegetable oil
1 small onion, chopped
1 garlic clove, crushed
2.5 cm/1 in piece root ginger, peeled and grated
15 ml/½ tbsp cornflour
300 ml/½ pint/1¼ cups light stock
30 ml/2 tbsp tomato purée
15 g/½ oz/1 tbsp soft dark brown sugar
30 ml/2 tbsp white wine vinegar
30 ml/2 tbsp rice wine or sherry
salt and pepper
cucumber, to garnish

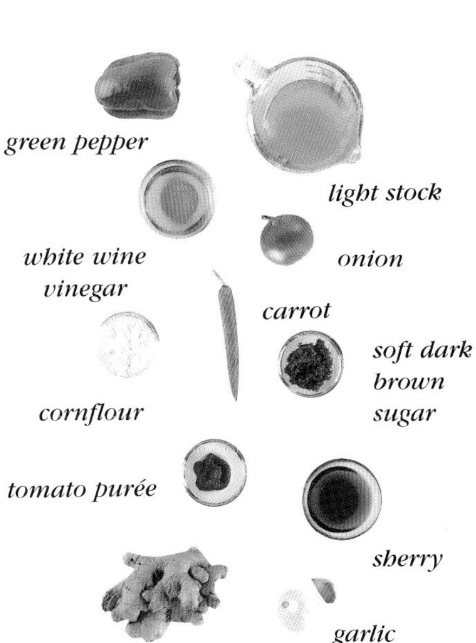

1 Peel the carrot and cut into matchstick-sized strips. Quarter the pepper, discard the stalks, seeds and membrane and cut into strips.

2 Heat the oil and fry the onion and garlic until soft but not brown. Add the carrot, pepper and ginger and cook for a further minute. Remove from the heat.

3 Blend the cornflour with a little stock and add to the vegetables, together with the remaining ingredients.

4 Stir over a moderate heat until the mixture boils and thickens. Simmer uncovered for 2–3 minutes until the vegetables are just tender. Adjust the seasoning and serve with strips of stir-fried pork or chicken and with rice or noodles.

NUTRITIONAL NOTES

PER PORTION:

ENERGY 85 Kcals/357 KJ **FAT** 3.0 g
SATURATED FAT 0.4 g **PROTEIN** 1.5 g
CARBOHYDRATE 12.6 g **FIBRE** 1.5 g

Tangy Orange Sauce (Sauce Bigarade)

A tangy orange sauce for roast duck and rich game. For a full mellow flavour it is best made with the rich roasting-pan juices – make sure that you pour off all the fat from the pan.

Serves 4 – 6

INGREDIENTS
roasting-pan juices
40 g/1½ oz/3 tbsp plain flour
300 ml/½ pint/1¼ cups hot stock (preferably duck)
150 ml/¼ pint/⅔ cup red wine
2 Seville oranges or 2 sweet oranges plus 10 ml/2 tsp lemon juice
15 ml/1 tbsp orange-flavoured liqueur
30 ml/2 tbsp redcurrant jelly
salt and pepper

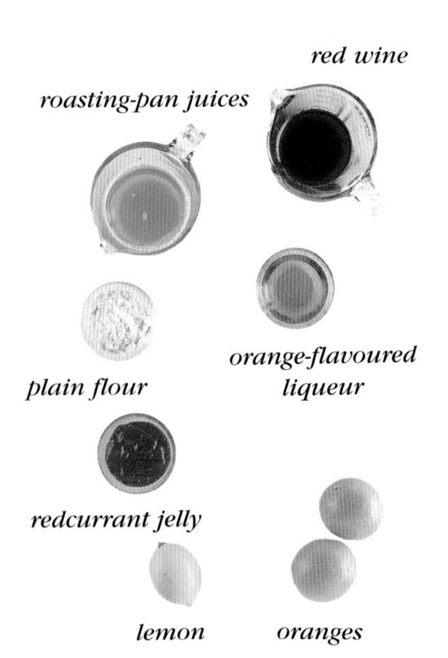

NUTRITIONAL NOTES
PER PORTION:
ENERGY 127 Kcals/533 KJ **FAT** 1.2 g
SATURATED FAT 0.4 g **PROTEIN** 2.2 g
CARBOHYDRATE 19.9 g **FIBRE** 1.3 g

1 Pour off any excess fat from the roasting pan, leaving the juices.

2 Sprinkle in the flour and cook, stirring continuously for 4 minutes or until lightly browned.

3 Off the heat, gradually blend in the hot stock and wine. Bring to the boil, stirring continuously. Lower the heat and simmer gently for 5 minutes.

4 Meanwhile, using a citrus zester, peel the rind thinly from one orange. Squeeze the juice from both oranges.

5 Blanch the rind; place it in a small pan, cover with water and bring to the boil. Cook for 5 minutes, drain and add the rind to the sauce.

6 Add the orange juice, liqueur and jelly to the sauce, stirring until the jelly has dissolved. Season to taste and pour over the jointed duckling or game.

Tomato Sauce with Gnocchi and Tagliatelle

Serves 4–6

INGREDIENTS
450 g/1 lb mixed flavoured tagliatelle
flour, for dusting
shavings of Parmesan cheese, to garnish

SPINACH GNOCCHI
450 g/1 lb frozen chopped spinach
1 small onion, finely chopped
1 garlic clove, crushed
1.5 ml/¼ tsp ground nutmeg
400 g/14 oz low-fat cottage cheese
115 g/4 oz dried white breadcrumbs
75 g/3 oz semolina or plain flour
50 g/2 oz grated Parmesan cheese
3 egg whites
salt and pepper

TOMATO SAUCE
1 onion, finely chopped
1 stick celery, finely chopped
1 red pepper, seeded and diced
1 garlic clove, crushed
150 ml/¼ pint/⅔ cup vegetable stock
400 g/14 oz can tomatoes
15 ml/1 tbsp tomato purée
10 ml/2 tsp caster sugar
5 ml/1 tsp dried oregano

1 To make the tomato sauce, put the chopped onion, celery, pepper and garlic into a non-stick pan. Add the stock, bring to the boil and cook for 5 minutes or until tender.

2 Add the tomatoes, tomato purée, sugar and oregano. Season to taste, bring to the boil and simmer for 30 minutes until thick, stirring occasionally.

3 Meanwhile, put the frozen spinach, onion and garlic into a saucepan, cover and cook until the spinach is defrosted. Remove the lid and increase the heat to drive off any moisture. Season with salt, pepper and nutmeg. Cool the spinach in a bowl, add the remaining ingredients and mix thoroughly.

4 Shape the mixture into about 24 ovals with two dessertspoons and place them on a lightly floured tray. Place in the fridge for 30 minutes.

5 Have a large shallow pan of boiling, salted water ready. Cook the gnocchi in batches, for about 5 minutes (the water should simmer gently and not boil). As soon as the gnocchi rise to the surface, remove them with a slotted spoon and drain thoroughly.

6 Cook the tagliatelle in a large pan of boiling, salted water until *al dente*. Drain thoroughly. Transfer to warmed serving plates, top with gnocchi and spoon over the tomato sauce. Scatter with shavings of Parmesan cheese and serve at once.

NUTRITIONAL NOTES

PER PORTION:

ENERGY 789Kcals/3315KJ **FAT** 10.9g
SATURATED FAT 3.7g **CHOLESTEROL** 20mg
CARBOHYDRATE 135g **FIBRE** 8.1g

Milanese Sauce with Tagliatelle

Serves 4

INGREDIENTS
1 onion, finely chopped
1 stick celery, finely chopped
1 red pepper, seeded and diced
1–2 garlic cloves, crushed
150 ml/¼ pint/⅔ cup vegetable stock
400 g/14 oz can tomatoes
15 ml/1 tbsp concentrated tomato purée
10 ml/2 tsp caster sugar
5 ml/1 tsp mixed dried herbs
350 g/12 oz tagliatelle
115 g/4 oz button mushrooms, sliced
60 ml/4 tbsp white wine
115 g/4 oz lean cooked ham, diced
salt and ground black pepper
15 ml/1 tbsp chopped fresh parsley, to garnish

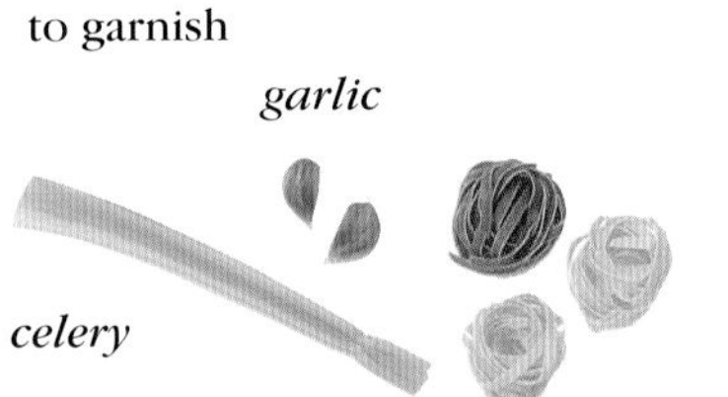

garlic
celery
tagliatelle
red pepper
onion

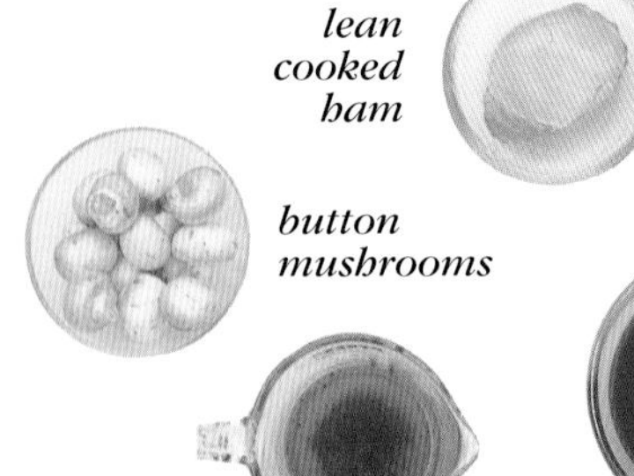

lean cooked ham
button mushrooms
vegetable stock

parsley
tomatoes
white wine
tomato purée

1 Put the chopped onion, celery, pepper and garlic into a non-stick pan. Add the stock, bring to the boil and cook for 5 minutes or until tender.

2 Add the tomatoes, tomato purée, sugar and herbs. Season with salt and pepper. Bring to the boil, simmer for 30 minutes until thick. Stir occasionally.

3 Cook the pasta in a large pan of boiling, salted water until *al dente*. Drain thoroughly.

4 Put the mushrooms into a pan with the white wine, cover and cook for 3–4 minutes until tender and all the wine has been absorbed.

5 Add the mushrooms and diced ham to the tomato sauce. Reheat gently.

6 Transfer the pasta to a warmed serving dish and spoon on the sauce. Garnish with parsley.

NUTRITIONAL NOTES
PER PORTION:

ENERGY 405Kcals/1700KJ **FAT** 3.5g
SATURATED FAT 0.8g **CHOLESTEROL** 17mg
CARBOHYDRATE 77g **FIBRE** 4.5g

Mixed Bean Chilli Sauce

Serves 6

Ingredients
1 onion, finely chopped
1–2 garlic cloves, crushed
1 large green chilli, seeded and chopped
150 ml/¼ pint/⅔ cup vegetable stock
400 g/14 oz can chopped tomatoes
30 ml/2 tbsp concentrated tomato purée
120 ml/4 fl oz/½ cup red wine
5 ml/1 tsp dried oregano
200 g/7 oz French beans, sliced
400 g/14 oz can red kidney beans, drained
400 g/14 oz can cannellini beans, drained
400 g/14 oz can chick-peas, drained
450 g/1 lb spaghetti
salt and ground black pepper

1 To make the sauce, put the chopped onion, garlic and chilli into a non-stick pan with the stock. Bring to the boil and cook for 5 minutes until tender.

2 Add the tomatoes, tomato purée, wine, seasoning and oregano. Bring to the boil, cover and simmer the sauce for 20 minutes.

Nutritional Notes

Per Portion:

Energy 431Kcals/1811KJ **Fat** 3.6g
Saturated Fat 0.2g **Cholesterol** 0mg
Carbohydrate 82g **Fibre** 9.9g

3 Cook the beans in boiling, salted water for about 5–6 minutes until tender. Drain thoroughly.

4 Add all the beans to the sauce and simmer for a further 10 minutes. Cook the spaghetti in a large pan of boiling, salted water until *al dente*. Drain thoroughly. Transfer to a serving dish and top with the chilli beans.

Black Olive and Mushroom Sauce with Spaghetti

A rich pungent sauce topped with sweet cherry tomatoes.

Serves 4

INGREDIENTS
5 ml/1 tsp olive oil
1 garlic clove, chopped
225 g/8 oz mushrooms, chopped
50 g/2 oz black olives, pitted
30 ml/2 tbsp chopped fresh parsley
1 fresh red chilli, seeded and chopped
450 g/1 lb spaghetti
225 g/8 oz cherry tomatoes
slivers of Parmesan cheese, to serve (optional)

1 Heat the oil in a large pan. Add the garlic and cook for 1 minute. Add the mushrooms, cover, and cook over a medium heat for 5 minutes.

2 Place the mushrooms in a blender or food processor with the olives, parsley and red chilli. Blend until smooth.

NUTRITIONAL NOTES
PER PORTION:
ENERGY 425 Kcals/1785 KJ **FAT** 4.7 g
SATURATED FAT 0.7 g **PROTEIN** 15.3 g
CARBOHYDRATE 85.6 g **FIBRE** 5.1 g

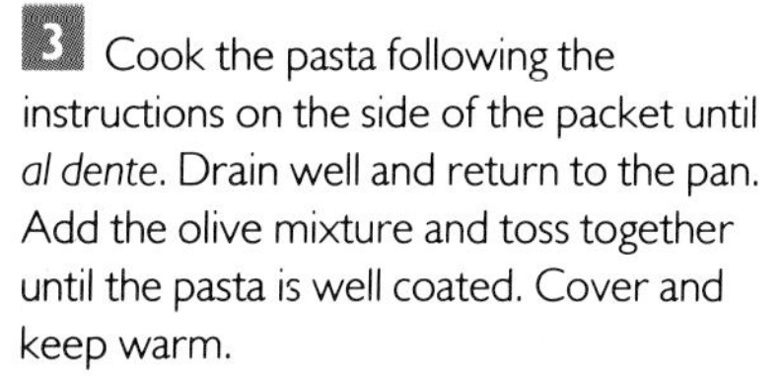

3 Cook the pasta following the instructions on the side of the packet until *al dente*. Drain well and return to the pan. Add the olive mixture and toss together until the pasta is well coated. Cover and keep warm.

4 Heat an ungreased frying pan and shake the cherry tomatoes around until they start to split (about 2–3 minutes). Serve the pasta topped with the tomatoes and garnished with slivers of Parmesan, if liked.

Creamy Pea Sauce with Pasta, Asparagus and Broad Beans

A creamy pea sauce makes a wonderful combination with crunchy young vegetables.

Serves 4

INGREDIENTS
15 ml/1 tbsp olive oil
1 garlic clove, crushed
6 spring onions, sliced
225 g/8 oz/1 cup frozen peas, defrosted
350 g/12 oz fresh young asparagus
30 ml/2 tbsp chopped fresh sage, plus extra leaves to garnish
finely grated rind of 2 lemons
450 ml/¾ pint/1¾ cups vegetable stock or water
225 g/8 oz frozen broad beans, defrosted
450 g/1 lb tagliatelle
60 ml/4 tbsp low-fat yogurt

1 Heat the oil in a pan. Add the garlic and spring onions and cook gently for 2–3 minutes until softened.

2 Add the peas and ⅓ of the asparagus, together with the sage, lemon rind and stock or water. Bring to the boil, reduce the heat and simmer for 10 minutes until tender. Purée in a blender until smooth.

3 Meanwhile remove the outer skins from the broad beans and discard.

4 Cut the remaining asparagus into 5 cm/2 in lengths trimming off any tough fibrous stems, and blanch in boiling water for 2 minutes.

5 Cook the tagliatelle following the instructions on the side of the packet until *al dente*. Drain well.

NUTRITIONAL NOTES

PER PORTION:

CALORIES 522 **FAT** 6.9 g
SATURATED FAT 0.9 g **PROTEIN** 23.8 g
CARBOHYDRATE 97.1 g **FIBRE** 11.2 g

COOK'S TIP

Frozen peas and beans have been used here to cut down the preparation time, but the dish tastes even better if you use fresh young vegetables when in season.

6 Add the cooked asparagus and shelled beans to the sauce and reheat. Stir in the yogurt and toss into the tagliatelle. Garnish with a few extra sage leaves and serve.

Provençal Sauce with Pappardelle

Serves 4

INGREDIENTS
2 small purple onions, peeled
150 ml/¼ pint/⅔ cup vegetable stock
1–2 garlic cloves, crushed
60 ml/4 tbsp red wine
2 courgettes, cut in fingers
1 yellow pepper, seeded and sliced
400 g/14 oz can tomatoes
10 ml/2 tsp fresh thyme
5 ml/1 tsp caster sugar
350 g/12 oz pappardelle
salt and ground black pepper
fresh thyme and 6 black olives, stoned and roughly chopped, to garnish

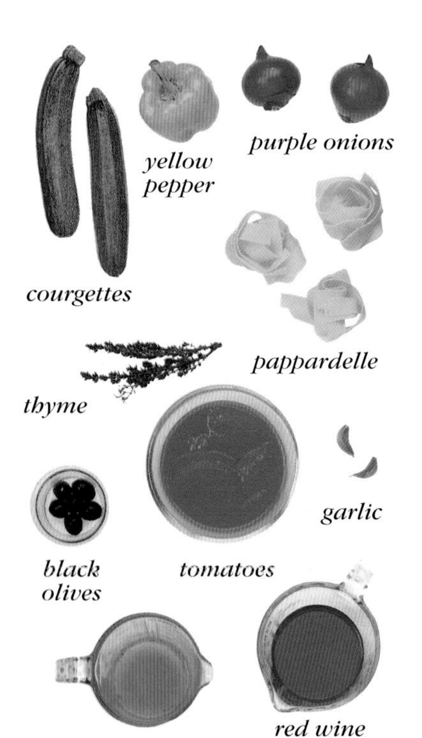

1 Cut each onion into eight wedges through the root end, to hold them together during cooking. Put into a saucepan with the stock and garlic. Bring to the boil, cover and simmer for 5 minutes until tender.

2 Add the red wine, courgettes, yellow pepper, tomatoes, thyme, sugar and seasoning. Bring to the boil and cook gently for 5–7 minutes, shaking the pan occasionally to coat the vegetables with the sauce. (Do not overcook the vegetables as they are much nicer if they are slightly crunchy.)

3 Cook the pasta in a large pan of boiling, salted water until *al dente*. Drain thoroughly.

4 Transfer the pasta to a warmed serving dish and top with the vegetables. Garnish with fresh thyme and chopped black olives.

NUTRITIONAL NOTES

PER PORTION:

ENERGY 369Kcals/1550KJ **FAT** 2.5g
SATURATED FAT 0.4g **CHOLESTEROL** 0mg
CARBOHYDRATE 75g **FIBRE** 4.3g

Tomato and Tuna Sauce with Pasta Shells

Serves 6

INGREDIENTS
1 medium onion, finely chopped
1 stick celery, finely chopped
1 red pepper, seeded and diced
1 garlic clove, crushed
150 ml/¼ pint/⅔ cup chicken stock
400 g/14 oz can chopped tomatoes
15 ml/1 tbsp tomato purée
10 ml/2 tsp caster sugar
15 ml/1 tbsp chopped fresh basil
15 ml/1 tbsp chopped fresh parsley
450 g/1 lb dried pasta shells
400 g/14 oz canned tuna in
brine, drained
30 ml/2 tbsp capers in
vinegar, drained
salt and ground black pepper

1 Put the chopped onion, celery, pepper and garlic into a non-stick pan. Add the stock, bring to the boil and cook for 5 minutes or until the stock has reduced almost completely.

2 Add the tomatoes, tomato purée, sugar and herbs. Season to taste and bring to the boil. Simmer for 30 minutes until thick, stirring occasionally.

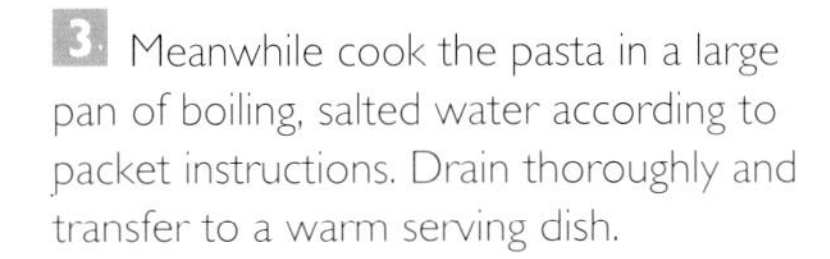

3 Meanwhile cook the pasta in a large pan of boiling, salted water according to packet instructions. Drain thoroughly and transfer to a warm serving dish.

4 Flake the tuna fish into large chunks and add to the sauce with the capers. Heat gently for 1–2 minutes, pour over the pasta, toss gently and serve at once.

NUTRITIONAL NOTES

PER PORTION:

ENERGY 369Kcals/1549KJ **FAT** 2.1g
SATURATED FAT 0.4g **CHOLESTEROL** 34mg
CARBOHYDRATE 65g **FIBRE** 4g

Bolognese Sauce with Ravioli

Serves 6

INGREDIENTS
225 g/8 oz low-fat cottage cheese
30 ml/2 tbsp grated Parmesan cheese, plus extra for serving
1 egg white, beaten, including extra for brushing
1.5 ml/1/4 tsp ground nutmeg
1 quantity of basic pasta dough
flour, for dusting
1 medium onion, finely chopped
1 garlic clove, crushed
150 ml/1/4 pint/2/3 cup beef stock
350 g/12 oz minced extra lean beef
120 ml/4 fl oz/1/2 cup red wine
30 ml/2 tbsp concentrated tomato purée
400 g/14 oz can chopped tomatoes
2.5 ml/1/2 tsp chopped fresh rosemary
1.5 ml/1/4 tsp ground allspice
salt and ground black pepper

1 To make the filling mix the cottage cheese, grated Parmesan, egg white, seasoning and nutmeg together thoroughly.

2 Roll the pasta into thin sheets, place a small teaspoon of filling along the pasta in rows 5 cm/2 in apart.

3 Moisten between the filling with beaten egg white. Lay a second sheet of pasta lightly over the top and press between each pocket to remove any air and seal firmly.

4 Cut into rounds with a fluted ravioli or pastry cutter. Transfer to a floured cloth and rest for at least 30 minutes before cooking.

5 To make the Bolognese sauce cook the onion and garlic in the stock for 5 minutes or until all the stock has reduced. Add the beef and cook quickly to brown, breaking up the meat with a fork. Add the wine, tomato purée, chopped tomatoes, rosemary and allspice, bring to the boil and simmer for 1 hour. Adjust the seasoning to taste.

6 Cook the ravioli in a large pan of boiling, salted water for 4–5 minutes. (Cook in batches to stop them sticking together). Drain thoroughly. Serve topped with Bolognese sauce. Serve grated Parmesan cheese separately.

NUTRITIONAL NOTES
PER PORTION:

ENERGY 321Kcals/1347KJ **FAT** 8.8g
SATURATED FAT 3.1g **CHOLESTEROL** 158mg
CARBOHYDRATE 32g **FIBRE** 2g

Cheese Sauce & Macaroni

Serves 4

INGREDIENTS

1 medium onion, chopped
150 ml/¼ pint/⅔ cup vegetable or chicken stock
25 g/1 oz low-fat margarine
40 g/1½ oz plain flour
300 ml/½ pint/¼ cup skimmed milk
50 g/2 oz reduced-fat Cheddar cheese, grated
5 ml/1 tsp mustard
225 g/8 oz quick-cook macaroni
4 smoked turkey rashers, cut in half
2–3 firm tomatoes, sliced
a few fresh basil leaves
15 ml/1 tbsp grated Parmesan cheese
salt and ground black pepper

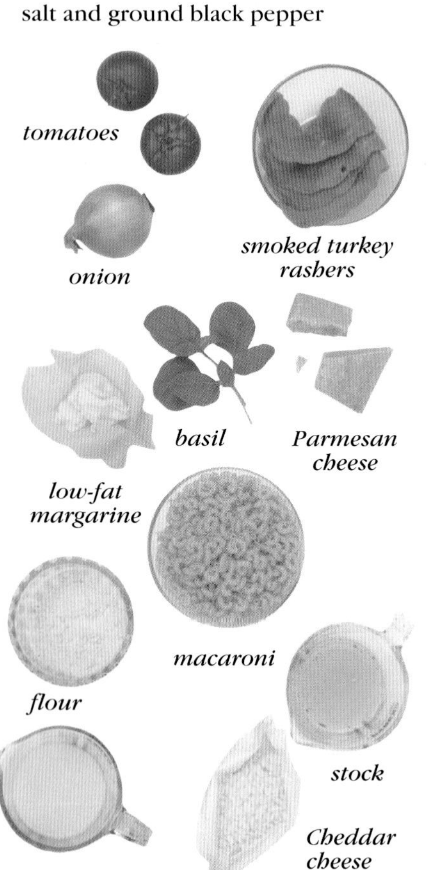

1 Put the onion and stock into a non-stick frying pan. Bring to the boil, stirring occasionally and cook for 5–6 minutes or until the stock has reduced entirely and the onions are transparent.

2 Put the margarine, flour, milk, and seasoning into a saucepan and whisk together over the heat until thickened and smooth. Draw aside and add the cheese, mustard and onions.

NUTRITIONAL NOTES

PER PORTION:

ENERGY 152Kcals/637KJ **FAT** 2.8g
SATURATED FAT 0.7g **CHOLESTEROL** 12mg
CARBOHYDRATE 23g **FIBRE** 1.1g

3 Cook the macaroni in a large pan of boiling, salted water for 6 minutes or according to the instructions on the packet. Drain thoroughly and stir into the sauce. Transfer the macaroni to a shallow ovenproof dish.

4 Arrange the turkey rashers and tomatoes so that they overlap on top of the macaroni cheese. Tuck the basil leaves over the tomatoes. Lightly sprinkle with Parmesan cheese and grill to lightly brown the top.

Watercress and Herb Sauce with Prawns and Pasta

Serves 4–6

INGREDIENTS
4 anchovy fillets, drained
60 ml/4 tbsp skimmed milk
225 g/8 oz squid
15 ml/1 tbsp chopped capers
15 ml/1 tbsp chopped gherkins
1–2 garlic cloves, crushed
150 ml/¼ pint/⅔ cup low-fat plain yogurt
30–45 ml/2–3 tbsp reduced-fat mayonnaise
squeeze of lemon juice
50 g/2 oz watercress, chopped finely
30 ml/2 tbsp chopped fresh parsley
30 ml/2 tbsp chopped fresh basil
350 g/12 oz fusilli
350 g/12 oz shelled prawns
salt and ground black pepper

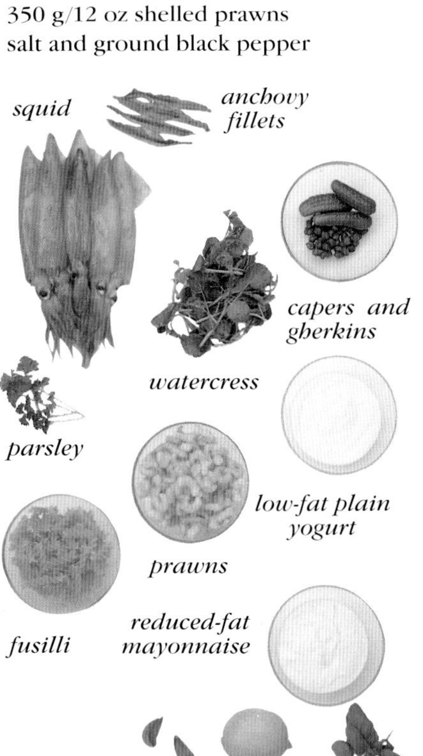

1 Put the anchovies into a small bowl and cover with the skimmed milk. Leave to soak for 10 minutes to remove the oil and strong salty flavour. Pull the head from the body of each squid and remove the quill. Peel outer speckled skin from the bodies. Cut the tentacles from the heads and rinse under cold water. Cut into 5 mm/¼ in rings.

2 To make the dressing, mix the capers, gherkins, garlic, yogurt, mayonnaise, lemon juice and fresh herbs in a bowl. Drain and chop the anchovies. Add to the dressing with the seasoning.

3 Drop the squid rings into a large pan of boiling, salted water. Lower the heat and simmer for 1–2 minutes (do not overcook or the squid will become tough). Remove with a slotted spoon. Cook the pasta in the same water according to the instructions on the packet. Drain thoroughly.

4 Mix the prawns and squid into the dressing in a large bowl. Add the pasta, toss and serve warm or cold as a salad.

NUTRITIONAL NOTES

PER PORTION:

ENERGY 502Kcals/2107KJ **FAT** 6.9g
SATURATED FAT 1.1g **CHOLESTEROL** 72mg
CARBOHYDRATE 71g **FIBRE** 3.2g

Spinach Sauce with Seafood Pasta Shells

You'll need very large pasta shells, measuring about 4 cm/1½ in long for this dish; don't try stuffing smaller shells – they're much too fiddly!

NUTRITIONAL NOTES

PER PORTION:

ENERGY 399 Kcals/1676 KJ **PROTEIN** 32.69 g
FAT 12.79 g **SATURATED FAT** 5.81 g
CARBOHYDRATE 40.75 g **FIBRE** 3.31 g
ADDED SUGAR 0 **SALT** 3.59 g

Serves 4

INGREDIENTS
- 15 g/½ oz/1 tbsp low fat spread
- 8 spring onions, finely sliced
- 6 tomatoes
- 32 large dried pasta shells
- 225 g/8 oz/1 cup low fat soft cheese
- 90 ml/6 tbsp skimmed milk
- pinch of freshly grated nutmeg
- 225 g/8 oz prawns
- 175 g/6 oz can white crabmeat, drained and flaked
- 115 g/4 oz frozen chopped spinach, thawed and drained
- salt and freshly ground black pepper

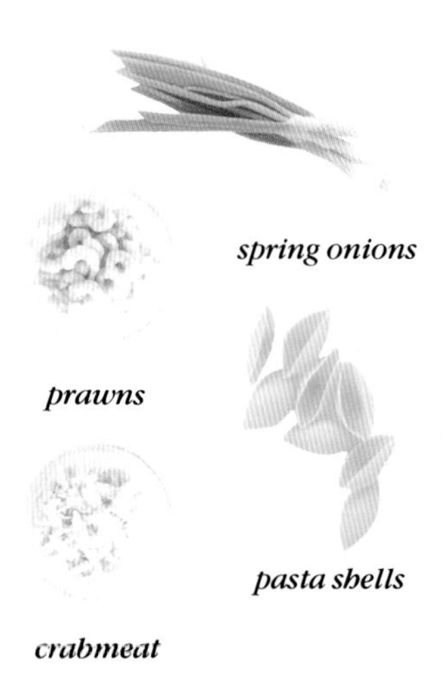

1 Pre-heat the oven to 150°C/300°F/Gas 2. Melt the low fat spread in a small saucepan and gently cook the spring onions for 3-4 minutes, or until softened.

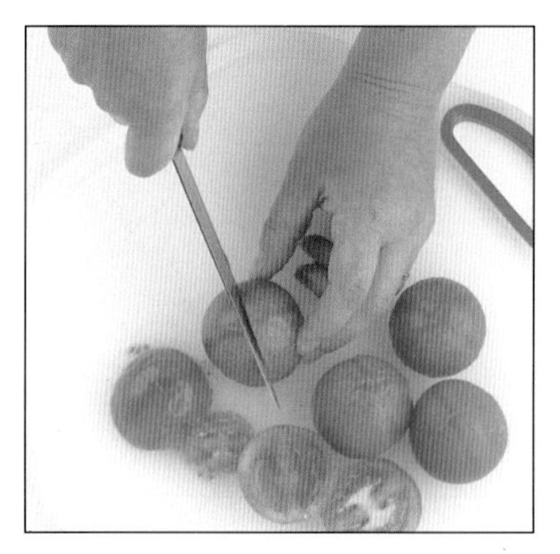

2 Plunge the tomatoes into a saucepan of boiling water for 1 minute, then into a saucepan of cold water. Slip off the skins. Halve the tomatoes, remove the seeds and cores and roughly chop the flesh.

3 Cook the pasta shells in lightly salted boiling water for about 10 minutes, or until *al dente*. Drain well.

4 Put the low fat soft cheese and skimmed milk into a saucepan and heat gently, stirring until blended. Season with salt, freshly ground black pepper and a pinch of nutmeg. Measure 30 ml/2 tbsp of the sauce into a bowl.

5 Add the spring onions, tomatoes, prawns, and crabmeat to the bowl. Mix well. Spoon the filling into the shells and place in a single layer in a shallow ovenproof dish. Cover with foil and cook in the pre-heated oven for 10 minutes.

6 Stir the spinach into the remaining sauce. Bring to the boil and simmer gently for 1 minute, stirring all the time. Drizzle over the pasta shells and serve hot.

Tomato Salsas

Salsa is Spanish for sauce, but elsewhere it has come to mean a side dish of finely chopped vegetables or fruits, which really enhances the meals it accompanies.

Serves 6

INGREDIENTS
6 medium tomatoes
1 green Kenyan chilli
2 spring onions, chopped
10 cm/4 in length cucumber, diced
30 ml/2 tbsp lemon juice
30 ml/2 tbsp fresh coriander, chopped
15 ml/1 tbsp fresh parsley, chopped
salt and pepper

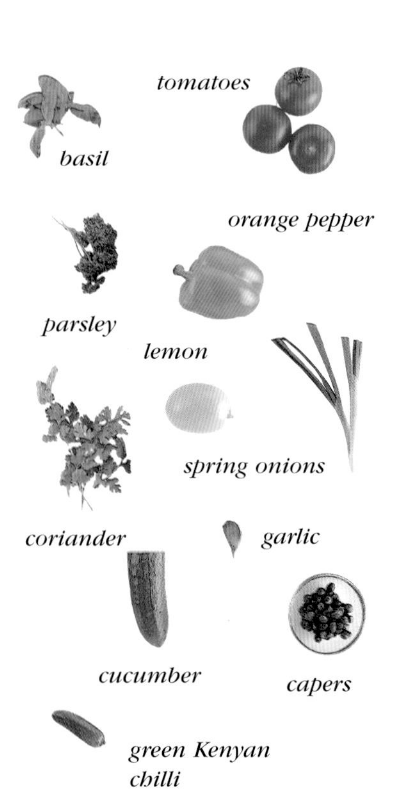

1 Cut a small cross in the stalk end of each tomato. Place in a bowl and cover with boiling water.

2 After 30 seconds or as soon as the skins split, drain and plunge into cold water. Gently slide off the skins. Quarter the tomatoes, remove the seeds and dice the flesh.

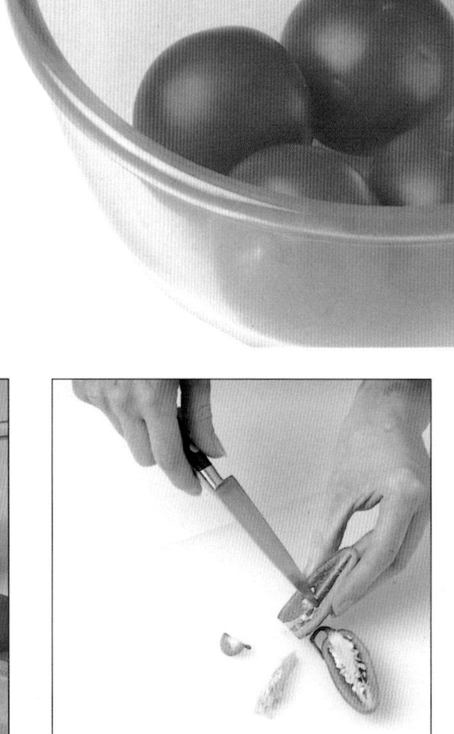

3 Halve the chilli, remove the stalk, seeds and membrane, and chop finely.

4 Mix together all the ingredients and transfer to a serving bowl. Chill for 1–2 hours before serving.

NUTRITIONAL NOTES

PER PORTION:

ENERGY 14 Kcals/61 KJ **FAT** 0.3 g
SATURATED FAT 0 **PROTEIN** 0.8 g
CARBOHYDRATE 2.4 g **FIBRE** 0.9 g

VARIATIONS

Tomato and Caper Salsa: Prepare the tomatoes and stir in the onion and lemon juice. Add six torn sprigs of basil and 15 ml/1 tbsp roughly chopped capers. Season to taste.

Tomato and Roast Pepper Salsa: Prepare 4 tomatoes and stir in the chilli, onion and herbs. Add a roasted, peeled and diced orange pepper and a crushed garlic clove. Season to taste.

Roasted Pepper and Ginger Salsa

Char-grilling to remove the skins will take away any bitterness from the peppers.

Serves 6

NUTRITIONAL NOTES

PER PORTION:

ENERGY 33 Kcals/138 KJ **FAT** 0.6 g
SATURATED FAT 0 **PROTEIN** 1.4 g
CARBOHYDRATE 5.9 g **FIBRE** 1.6 g

INGREDIENTS

1 large red pepper
1 large yellow pepper
1 large orange pepper
2.5 cm/1 in piece root ginger
2.5 ml/½ tsp coriander seeds
5 ml/1 tsp cumin seeds
1 small garlic clove
30 ml/2 tbsp lime or lemon juice
1 small red onion, finely chopped
30 ml/2 tbsp chopped fresh coriander
5 ml/1 tsp chopped fresh thyme
salt and pepper

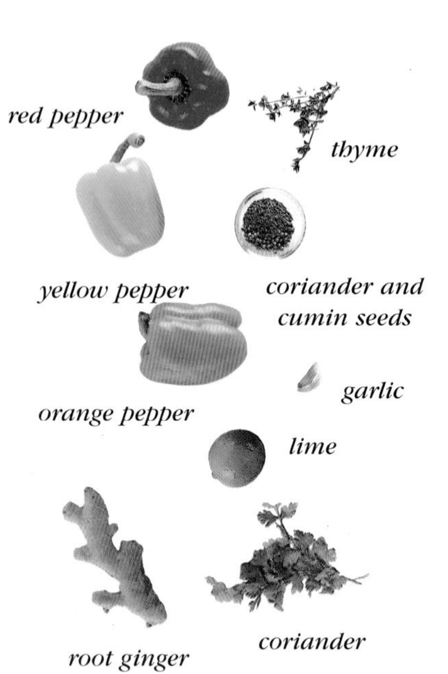

1 Quarter the peppers and remove the stalk, seeds and membranes.

2 Grill the quarters, skin side up, until charred and blistered. Rub away the skins and slice very finely.

3 Peel or scrape the root ginger and chop roughly.

4 Over a moderate heat, gently dry-fry the spices for 30 seconds to 1 minute, making sure they don't scorch.

5 Crush the spices in a pestle and mortar. Add the ginger and garlic and continue to work to a pulp. Work in the lime or lemon juice.

6 Mix together the peppers, spice mixture, onion and herbs. Season to taste and spoon into a serving bowl. Chill for 1–2 hours before serving as an accompaniment to barbecued meats or kebabs.

Melon and Chilli Salsa with Grilled Chicken

This dish originates from Mexico. Its hot fruity flavours form the essence of Tex-Mex cooking.

Serves 4

NUTRITIONAL NOTES

PER PORTION:

ENERGY 184 Kcals/774 KJ **FAT** 5.5 g
SATURATED FAT 1.4 g **PROTEIN** 25.7 g
CARBOHYDRATE 8.6 g **FIBRE** 0.8 g

INGREDIENTS
4 chicken breasts
pinch of celery salt and cayenne pepper combined
10 ml/2 tsp vegetable oil
corn chips, to serve

FOR THE SALSA
275 g/10 oz watermelon
175 g/6 oz canteloupe melon
1 small red onion
1–2 green chillies
30 ml/2 tbsp lime juice
60 ml/4 tbsp chopped fresh coriander
pinch of salt

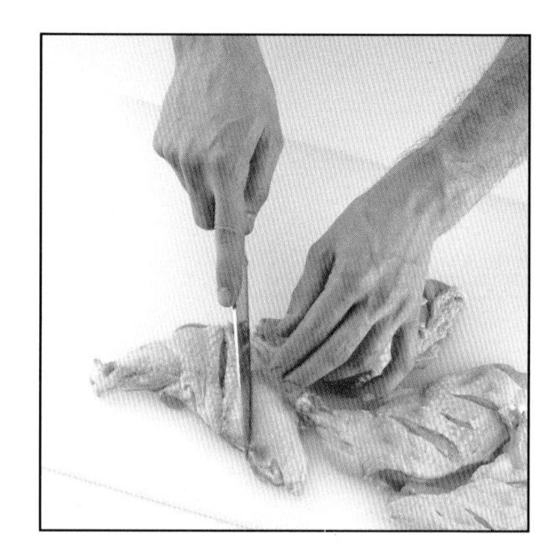

1 Preheat a moderate grill. Slash the chicken breasts deeply to speed up the cooking time.

2 Season the chicken with celery salt and cayenne, brush with oil and grill for about 15 minutes.

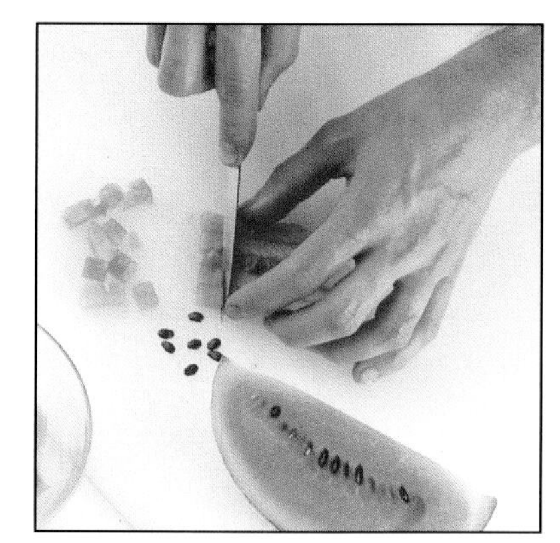

3 To make the salsa, remove the rind and as many seeds as you can from the melons. Finely dice the flesh and put it into a bowl.

4 Finely chop the onion, split the chillies (discarding the seeds which contain most of the heat) and chop. Take care not to touch sensitive skin areas when handling cut chillies. Mix with the melon.

5 Add the lime juice and chopped coriander, and season with a pinch of salt. Turn the salsa into a small bowl.

6 Arrange the grilled chicken on a plate and serve with the salsa and a handful of corn chips.

Fiery Citrus Salsa

This very unusual salsa makes a fantastic marinade for shellfish and it is also delicious drizzled over barbecued meat.

NUTRITIONAL NOTES

PER PORTION:

ENERGY 30 Kcals/127 KJ **FAT** 0.1 g
SATURATED FAT 0 **PROTEIN** 0.7 g
CARBOHYDRATE 7.1 g **FIBRE** 1.3 g

Serves 4

INGREDIENTS
1 orange
1 green apple
2 fresh red chillies
1 garlic clove
8 fresh mint leaves
juice of 1 lemon
salt and pepper

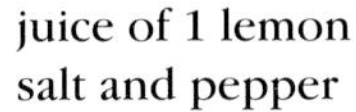

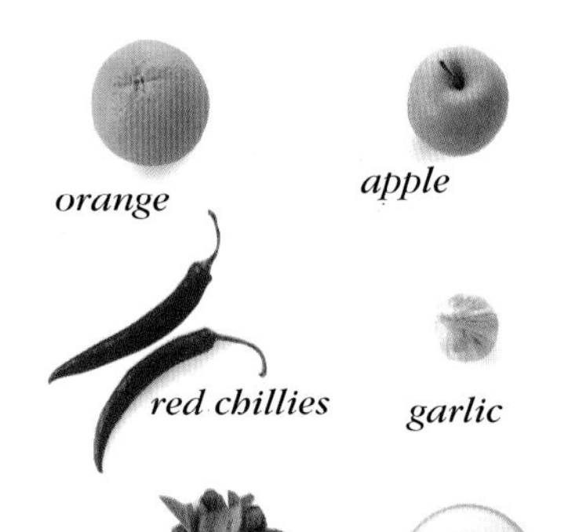

1 Slice the bottom off the orange so that it will stand firmly on a chopping board. Using a sharp knife, remove the peel by slicing from the top to the bottom of the orange.

2 Hold the orange in one hand over a bowl. Slice towards the middle of the fruit, to one side of a segment, and then gently twist the knife to ease the segment away from the membrane and out of the orange. Repeat to remove all the segments. Squeeze any juice from the remaining membrane into the bowl.

3 Peel the apple, slice it into wedges and remove the core.

4 Halve the chillies and remove their seeds, then place them in a blender or food processor with the orange segments and juice, apple wedges, garlic and fresh mint.

5 Process until smooth. Then, with the motor running, pour in the lemon juice.

6 Season to taste with a little salt and pepper. Pour into a bowl or small jug and serve immediately.

VARIATION

If you're feeling really fiery, don't seed the chillies! They will make the salsa particularly hot and fierce.

Aromatic Peach and Cucumber Salsa

Angostura bitters add an unusual and very pleasing flavour to this salsa. Distinctive, sweet-tasting mint complements chicken and other main meat dishes.

Serves 4

INGREDIENTS
2 peaches
1 mini cucumber
2.5 ml/½ tsp Angostura bitters
15 ml/1 tbsp olive oil
10 ml/2 tsp fresh lemon juice
30 ml/2 tbsp chopped fresh mint
salt and pepper

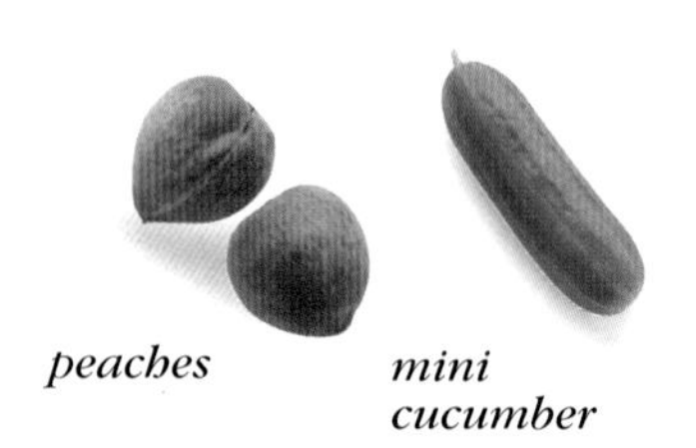

Angostura bitters *olive oil*

COOK'S TIP

The texture of the peach and the crispness of the cucumber will fade fairly rapidly, so try to prepare this salsa as close to serving time as possible.

1 Using a small sharp knife, carefully score a line right around the

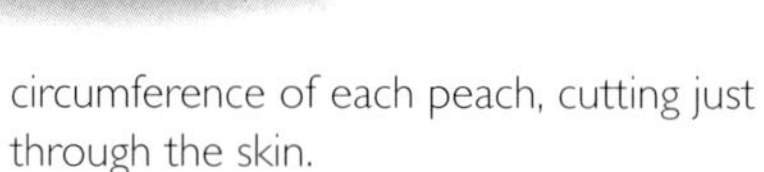

circumference of each peach, cutting just through the skin.

2 Bring a large pan of water to the boil. Add the peaches and blanch them for 60 seconds. Drain and briefly refresh in cold water.

3 Peel off and discard the skin. Halve the peaches and remove their stones. Finely dice the flesh and place in a bowl.

4 Trim the ends off the cucumber, then finely dice the flesh and stir it into the peaches.

5 Stir the Angostura bitters, olive oil and lemon juice together and then stir this dressing into the peach mixture.

NUTRITIONAL NOTES

PER PORTION:

ENERGY 47 Kcals/197 KJ **FAT** 2.9 g
SATURATED FAT 0.4 g **PROTEIN** 0.9 g
CARBOHYDRATE 4.8 g **FIBRE** 0.9 g

6 Stir in the mint with salt and pepper to taste. Chill and serve within 1 hour.

Mango and Red Onion Salsa

A very simple salsa, which is livened up by the addition of passion-fruit pulp.

NUTRITIONAL NOTES

PER PORTION:

ENERGY 61 Kcals/255 KJ **FAT** 0.3 g
SATURATED FAT 0 **PROTEIN** 1.1 g
CARBOHYDRATE 14.5 g **FIBRE** 2.9 g

Serves 4

INGREDIENTS
1 large ripe mango
1 red onion
2 passion fruit
6 large fresh basil leaves
juice of 1 lime, to taste
sea salt

mango

red onion

passion fruit

basil

lime juice

1 Holding the mango upright on a chopping board, use a large knife to slice the flesh away from either side of the large flat stone in two portions.

2 Using a smaller knife, trim away any flesh still clinging to the top and bottom of the stone.

3 Score the flesh of the mango halves deeply, taking care to avoid cutting through the skin: make parallel incisions about 1 cm/½ in apart; turn and cut lines in the opposite direction. Carefully turn the skin inside out so the flesh stands out like hedgehog spikes. Slice the dice away from the skin.

4 Finely chop the red onion and place it in a bowl with the mango.

5 Halve the passion fruit, scoop out the seeds and pulp, and add to the mango mixture.

6 Tear the basil leaves coarsely and stir them into the salsa with lime juice and a little sea salt to taste. Serve immediately.

VARIATION

Sweetcorn kernels are a delicious addition to this salsa.

Hot Plum Sauce with Floating Islands

An unusual, low fat pudding that is simpler to make than it looks. The plum sauce can be made in advance, then reheated just before you cook the meringues.

NUTRITIONAL NOTES

PER PORTION:

ENERGY 91 Kcals/380 KJ **FAT** 0.3 g
SATURATED FAT 0 **PROTEIN** 2.1 g
CARBOHYDRATE 21.2 g **FIBRE** 1.7 g

Serves 4

INGREDIENTS
450 g/1 lb red plums
300 ml/½ pint/1¼ cups apple juice
2 egg whites
30 ml/2 tbsp concentrated apple-juice syrup
freshly grated nutmeg

apple juice
red plums
eggs
concentrated apple-juice syrup
nutmeg

1 Halve the plums and remove the stones. Place them in a wide pan, with the apple juice.

2 Bring to the boil and then cover with a lid and leave to simmer gently until the plums are tender.

3 Meanwhile, place the egg whites in a clean, dry bowl and whisk them until they hold soft peaks.

4 Gradually whisk in the apple juice syrup, whisking until the meringue holds fairly firm peaks.

5 Using a tablespoon, scoop the meringue mixture into the gently simmering plum sauce. You may need to cook the 'islands' in two batches.

6 Cover and allow to simmer gently for 2–3 minutes, until the meringues are just set. Serve straight away, sprinkled with a little freshly grated nutmeg.

Apricot Sauce with Coconut Dumplings

These delicate little dumplings are very simple to make and cook in minutes. The sharp flavour of the sauce offsets the creamy dumplings beautifully.

Serves 4

Ingredients
For the dumplings
75 g/3 oz/⅓ cup cottage cheese
1 egg white
30 ml/2 tbsp low fat spread
15 ml/1 tbsp light muscovado sugar
30 ml/2 tbsp self-raising wholemeal flour
finely grated rind of ½ lemon
30 ml/2 tbsp desiccated coconut, toasted

For the sauce
225 g/8 oz can apricot halves in natural juice
15 ml/1 tbsp lemon juice

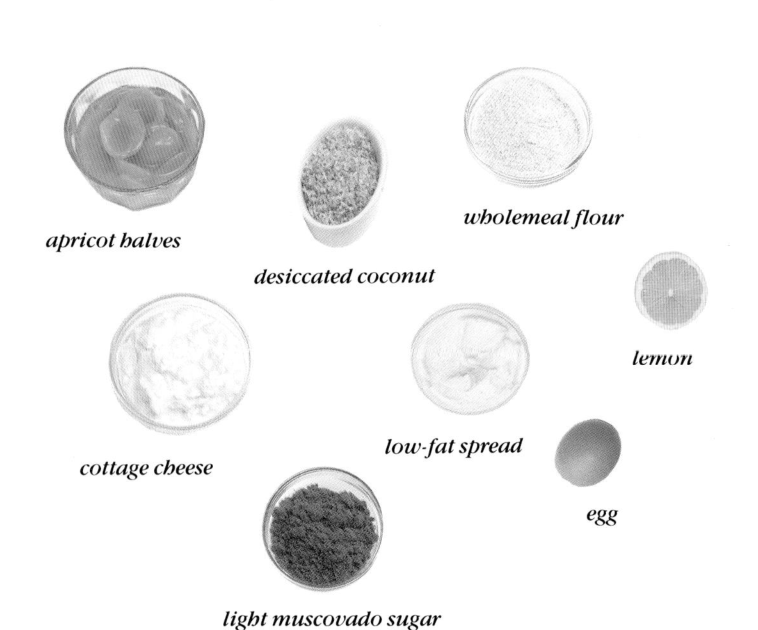

1 Half-fill a steamer with boiling water and put it on to boil. Alternatively, place a heatproof plate over a pan of boiling water.

2 Beat together the cottage cheese, egg white and low-fat spread until they are evenly mixed.

3 Stir in the sugar, flour, lemon rind and coconut, mixing everything evenly to a fairly firm dough.

4 Place 8–12 spoonfuls of the mixture in the steamer or on the plate, leaving a space between them.

NUTRITIONAL NOTES

PER PORTION:

ENERGY 136 Kcals/569 KJ **FAT** 7.4 g
SATURATED FAT 4.2 g **PROTEIN** 5.2 g
CARBOHYDRATE 13.0 g **FIBRE** 1.9 g

5 Cover the steamer or pan tightly with a lid or a plate and steam for about 10 minutes, until the dumplings have risen and are firm to the touch.

6 Meanwhile, purée the can of apricots and stir in the lemon juice. Pour into a small pan and heat until boiling, then serve with the dumplings. Sprinkle with extra coconut to serve.

Nectarine Sauce with Latticed Peaches

An elegant dessert; it certainly doesn't look low in fat, but it really is.

NUTRITIONAL NOTES

PER PORTION:

ENERGY 202 Kcals/851 KJ **FAT** 10.8 g
SATURATED FAT 4.3 g **PROTEIN** 4.9 g
CARBOHYDRATE 23.1 g **FIBRE** 2.3 g

Serves 6

INGREDIENTS

FOR THE PASTRY

115 g/4 oz/1 cup plain flour
45 ml/3 tbsp butter or sunflower margarine
45 ml/3 tbsp low-fat natural yogurt
30 ml/2 tbsp orange juice
skimmed milk

FOR THE FILLING

3 ripe peaches or nectarines
45 ml/3 tbsp ground almonds
30 ml/2 tbsp low-fat natural yogurt
finely grated rind of 1 small orange
1.25 ml/¼ tsp natural almond essence

FOR THE SAUCE

1 ripe peach or nectarine
45 ml/3 tbsp orange juice

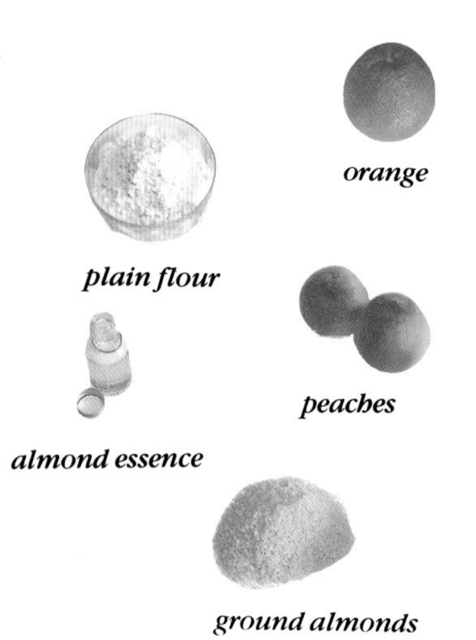

1 For the pastry, sift the flour into a bowl and, using your fingertips, rub in the butter or margarine evenly. Stir in the yogurt and orange juice to bind the mixture to a firm dough.

2 Roll out about half the pastry thinly and use a biscuit cutter to stamp out rounds about 7.5 cm/3 in in diameter, slightly larger than the circumference of the peaches. Place on a lightly greased baking sheet.

3 Skin the peaches, halve and remove the stones. Mix together the almonds, yogurt, orange rind and almond essence. Spoon into the hollows of each peach half and place, cut side down, on to the pastry rounds.

4 Roll out the remaining pastry thinly and cut into thin strips. Arrange the strips over the peaches to form a lattice, brushing with milk to secure firmly. Trim off the ends neatly.

5 Chill in the refrigerator for 30 minutes. Preheat the oven to 200°C/400°F/Gas 6. Brush with milk and bake for 15–18 minutes, until golden brown.

6 For the sauce, skin the peach or nectarine and halve it to remove the stone. Place the flesh in a food processor, with the orange juice, and purée it until smooth. Serve the peaches hot, with the peach sauce spooned around.

Lemon and Lime Sauce

A tangy, refreshing sauce to end a heavy meal, it goes well with pancakes or fruit tarts.

Serves 4

INGREDIENTS
1 lemon
2 limes
50 g/2 oz/¼ cup caster sugar
25 ml/1½ tbsp arrowroot
300 ml/½ pint/1¼ cups water
lemon balm or mint, to garnish

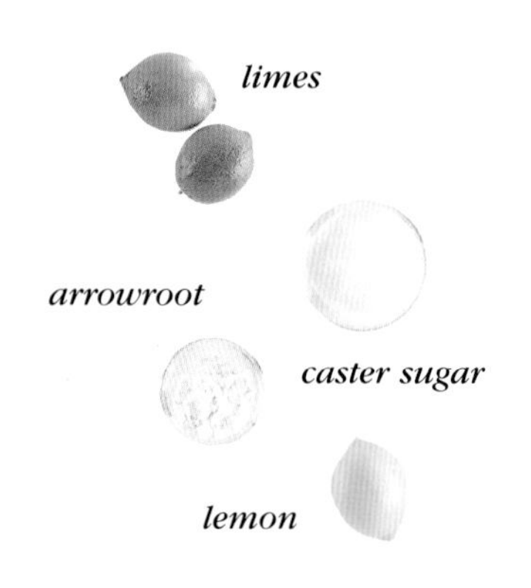

1 Using a citrus zester, peel the rinds thinly from the lemon and limes. Squeeze the juice from the fruit.

2 Place the rind in a pan, cover with water and bring to the boil. Drain through a sieve and reserve the rind.

3 In a small bowl, mix a little sugar with the arrowroot. Blend in enough water to give a smooth paste. Heat the remaining water, pour in the arrowroot, and stir continuously until the sauce boils and thickens.

4 Stir in the remaining sugar, citrus juice and reserved rind, and serve hot with freshly made pancakes. Decorate with lemon balm or mint.

VARIATION

This sauce can also be made with orange and lemon rind if you prefer, and makes an ideal accompaniment for a rich orange or mandarin cheesecake.

NUTRITIONAL NOTES

PER PORTION:

ENERGY 75 Kcals/317 KJ **FAT** 0.1 g
SATURATED FAT 0 **PROTEIN** 0.3 g
CARBOHYDRATE 19.6 g **FIBRE** 0

Raspberry Sauce with Baked Peaches

This tart fat-free fruit coulis is exceedingly quick to make – add a little liqueur for a special occasion.

Serves 4

INGREDIENTS
25 g/1 oz low fat spread, at room temperature
50 g/2 oz caster sugar
1 small egg, beaten
50 g/2 oz crushed amaretti biscuits
6 ripe peaches

FOR THE SAUCE
115 g/4 oz/1 cup raspberries
15 ml/1 tbsp icing sugar
15 ml/1 tbsp fruit-flavoured brandy (optional)

NUTRITIONAL NOTES
PER PORTION:

ENERGY 170 Kcals/712.5 KJ **FAT** 7.4 g
SATURATED FAT 1.1 g **PROTEIN** 4.4 g
CARBOHYDRATE 22 g **FIBRE** 2.7 g

1 Preheat the oven to 180°C/350°F/Gas 4. Beat the low fat spread with the sugar until soft and fluffy. Beat in the egg. Add the crushed amaretti biscuits and beat just to blend well together.

2 Halve the peaches and remove the stones. With a spoon, scrape out some of the flesh from each peach half, slightly enlarging the hollow left by the pit. Reserve the excess peach flesh to use in the sauce.

3 Place the peach halves on a baking sheet (if necessary, secure with crumpled foil to keep them steady). Fill the hollow in each peach half with a little of the amaretti mixture.

4 Bake for about 30 minutes until the filling is puffed and golden and the peaches are very tender.

5 Meanwhile, to make the sauce, combine all the ingredients in a food processor or blender. Add the reserved peach flesh. Process until smooth. Press through a sieve set over a bowl to remove fibres and seeds. Let the peaches cool slightly. Place 2 peach halves on each plate and spoon round some of the sauce. Serve immediately.

Maple-yogurt Sauce with Poached Pears

An elegant dessert that is easier to make than it looks – poach the pears in advance, and have the yogurt sauce ready to spoon on to the plates just before you serve.

Serves 4

Ingredients
For the pastry
6 firm dessert pears
15 ml/1 tbsp lemon juice
250 ml/8 fl oz/1 cup sweet white wine or cider
thinly pared rind of 1 lemon
1 cinnamon stick
30 ml/2 tbsp maple syrup
2.5ml/½ tsp arrowroot
150 g/5 oz/⅔ cup Greek yogurt

Nutritional Notes
Per portion:
Energy 128 Kcals/537 KJ **Fat** 2.4 g
Saturated Fat 1.4 g **Protein** 2.0 g
Carbohydrate 18.3 g **Fibre** 1.6 g

1 Thinly peel the pears, leaving them whole and with stalks. Brush them with lemon juice, to prevent them from browning. Use a potato peeler or small knife to scoop out the core from the base of each pear.

2 Place the pears in a wide, heavy pan and pour over the wine, with enough cold water almost to cover the pears.

3 Add the lemon rind and cinnamon stick, and then bring to the boil. Reduce the heat, cover the pan and simmer the pears gently for 30–40 minutes, or until tender. Turn the pears occasionally so that they cook evenly. Lift out the pears carefully, draining them well.

4 Bring the liquid to the boil and boil uncovered to reduce to about 100 ml/4 fl oz/½ cup. Strain and add the maple syrup. Blend a little of the liquid with the arrowroot. Return to the pan and cook, stirring, until thick and clear. Cool.

5 Slice each pear about three-quarters of the way through, leaving the slices attached at the stem end. Fan each pear out on a serving plate.

6 Stir 30 ml/2 tbsp of the cooled syrup into the yogurt and spoon it around the pears. Drizzle with the remaining syrup and serve immediately.

Strawberry Sauce with Lemon Hearts

This speedy sweet sauce is totally fat free and makes a delicious accompaniment for these delicate lemon-flavoured cheese hearts.

Serves 4

INGREDIENTS
175 g/6 oz/¾ cup ricotta cheese
150 ml/¼ pint/⅔ cup low fat yogurt
15 ml/1 tbsp granulated sweetener
finely grated rind of ½ lemon
30 ml/2 tbsp lemon juice
10 ml/2 tsp powdered gelatine
2 egg whites

FOR THE SAUCE
225 g/8 oz/2 cups fresh or frozen and thawed strawberries
15 ml/1 tbsp lemon juice

crème fraîche

ricotta cheese

powdered gelatine

lemon

strawberries

eggs

granulated sweetener

1 Beat the ricotta cheese until smooth. Stir in the low fat yogurt, sweetener and lemon rind.

2 Place the lemon juice in a small bowl and sprinkle the gelatine over it. Place the bowl over a pan of hot water and stir to dissolve the gelatine completely.

3 Quickly stir the gelatine into the cheese mixture, mixing it in evenly.

4 Beat the egg whites until they form soft peaks. Quickly fold them into the cheese mixture.

5 Spoon the mixture into six lightly oiled, individual heart-shaped moulds and chill the moulds until set.

NUTRITIONAL NOTES

PER PORTION:

ENERGY 86 Kcals/361 KJ **FAT** 3.5 g
SATURATED FAT 0.1 g **PROTEIN** 6.7 g
CARBOHYDRATE 7.5 g **FIBRE** 0.4 g

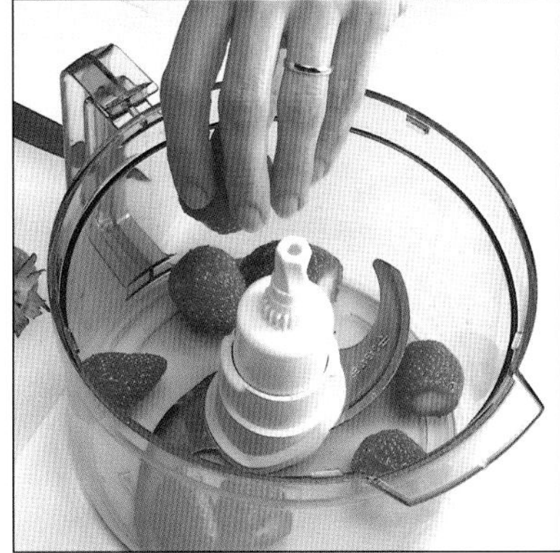

6 Place the strawberries and lemon juice in a blender and process until smooth. Pour the sauce on to serving plates and place the turned-out hearts on top. Decorate with slices of strawberry.

Redcurrant and Raspberry Coulis

A dessert sauce for the height of summer to serve with light meringues and fruit sorbets. Make it particularly pretty with a decoration of fresh flowers and leaves.

NUTRITIONAL NOTES

PER PORTION:

ENERGY 81 Kcals/340 KJ **FAT** 1.2 g
SATURATED FAT 0.6 g **PROTEIN** 1.7 g
CARBOHYDRATE 17.1 g **FIBRE** 3.2 g

Serves 6

INGREDIENTS
225 g/8 oz redcurrants
450 g/1 lb raspberries
50 g/2 oz/¹/₄ cup icing sugar
15 ml/1 tbsp cornflour
juice of 1 orange
30 ml/2 tbsp double cream

orange

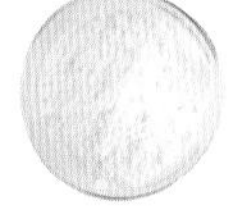

icing sugar

double cream

cornflour

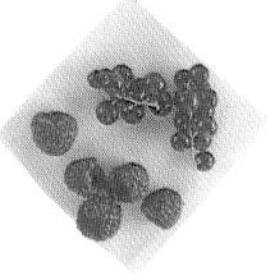

redcurrants and raspberries

1 Strip the redcurrants from their stalks using a fork. Place in a food processor or blender with the raspberries and sugar, and purée until it is smooth.

2 Press the mixture through a fine sieve into a bowl and discard the seeds and pulp.

3 Blend the cornflour with the orange juice then stir into the fruit purée. Transfer to a saucepan and bring to the boil, stirring continuously, and cook for 1–2 minutes until smooth and thick. Leave until cold.

4 Spoon the sauce over each plate. Drip the cream from a teaspoon to make small dots evenly around the edge. Draw a cocktail stick through the dots to form heart shapes. Scoop or spoon sorbet into the middle and decorate with flowers.

INDEX